BEC‌ING
FROM
THE
LIGHT

Exorcism, Clearing, and
Healing Prayers

Kass Huff, Psychic Medium

ISBN# 978-0-692-79926-0

Self-Published by Kass Huff
Manufactured in the United States of America
Pictures by Free Art, and Artist/Shutterstock.com

Proofread and edited by Larry Pratt 253-845-1043

For information about bulk purchases and discounts available
to retailers, please contact info@kasshuff.com.

Disclaimer
I am not a Doctor and these signs and symptoms of haunting and
possession are for the purpose of healing a haunting, or a person
experiencing a haunting or a possession and are not a medical
diagnosis (or to be used as such) or to be used in place of any
medical treatment. For any medical emergency call 911. For any
physical sickness call a Doctor. Check with your Doctor or
Primary Care Physician before using any herbs or burning any
herbs or starting any new healthcare routine.

This book is dedicated in Thanks firstly to

Creator,

in whom all things are possible,
and secondly to everyone who has and is now
supporting the Spiritual work of Jesus Christ.

Acknowledgements

To my Dad, Joseph Carlson who as I wrote this book was in his last days—said to me in his lowest time "isn't it a beautiful day? Isn't it beautiful to be alive"? This book is dedicated to you, Dad—through your love and kindness, I have come to experience the joyful love of a father. In my Father's last days, he taught me what strength and Faith really look like. I am forever grateful, I am forever blessed.

To my Mom, Helen Carlson (in Heaven) this book is possible because of all you invested lovingly in me, gave life to me, and raising me in the spiritual awareness of God. Thank you for all you taught me about love—through your love, deep compassion, and your light.

To my husband Adam Huff, thank you. Your support of my calling is a gift I wasn't prepared to receive and cherish now more than you know. Thank you for your love.

To my delightful and always wondrous children Lottie, Devin, Rosalynn, and Jeremy—may you be eternally blessed! Thank you for the love, support, and assistance you offered. Special thanks to Devin—for saying the original cover 'looks like Heaven'—and for showing me the true meaning of hope. Special thanks to Lottie—for your ability to ground me and help me see the bigger picture, I have so much gratitude for our relationship, and our friendship.

A special Thanks to my Elders—for without you I don't know who I would be today. Thank you to Jacque Martinson, Mike Lee, Sam Yellowbird, Lou J. Free and Sam, Grandmother Carmen Looking Horse, Kastasha, Sandie McNaughton, Dorothy Lynn, Rainbow Thunder Heart aka Benny LaBeau, Pat Rasmussen, Camille Moritz, White Eagle Medicine Woman, and Dr. John Hill. There are so many others, my head swims—know if you are not mentioned here (and you should be) you are forever in my heart with gratitude.

Grateful Thanks to everyone who offered spiritual support during the writing of this book, especially White Wolf for your stories of the turtle.

Deep thanks to the students and clients I have worked with that gave life and meaning to the prayers and teachings, and what you've taught me and others through your powerful desire to heal.

Contents

Acknowledgments...5

Foreword...13

Becoming from The Light 23

God's Light 35

What is a Haunting..39

Signs and Symptoms of a Haunting 43

The Process of Going to Heaven.........................50

What is a Demon... 62

What is a Possession...70

Two Forms of a Possession................................71

The 4 Most Common Reasons............................72

Signs and Symptoms of an External Possession.,.........74

Signs and Symptoms of an Internal Possession.........76

All Cords Must Be Cut.....................................81

Boundaries Need to Be Set in Place......................83

What is an Exorcism..86

Forgiveness and Deliverance..............................94

Exorcism Prayer...98

Ethical Wisdom.. 102

Part One: A Call For The Light................................104

Part Two: Opening An Extraction Vortex...................105

Part Three: Bringing A Soul To Light......................106

Part Four: Cancelling All Unholy Legal Rights.............108

Part Five: The Exorcism 111

Part Six: Cutting Of Cords..................................124

Part Seven: Spiritual Healing...............................126

Part Eight: Restoring God's Blessings.......................130

Part Nine: Rejoicing In The Light.......................... 131

To The Hollow Bone...133

Clearing Prayers...134

When and How to Clear a House.......................... 137

Prayers to Keep a Home Clear................................. 146

Prayers to Keep a Person Clear...............................148

Binding the Ahab, Jezebel, Succubus, Incubus..............150

Binding the Ahab, Jezebel, Succubus, Incubus Prayer......152

Removing Malevolent Ruler Spirits of a Person...............154

Removing Malevolent Ruler Spirits of a Place................. 155

Claiming God In Your Life……..……………....………156

Negative Blocks of Issue…………………………....……157

The Lighted 13……………………………………...……158

Colors…………………………………………...……..159

Spirit Fire……………………………………………. 159

Into the Violet Light……………………….………… 159

Healing Prayers………………….………………....160

Emotional Release Prayer………………….....…..……….. 162

Karmic Clearing Prayer…………………………...…. 168

I Release Prayer………………………………....………. 170

Heal me at the Root Jesus………………...…………... 171

My True Nature (suicide prevention prayer)………….. ... 172

I am a Butterfly…………………………………………. 173

Positive……………………………………………..… 174

Taking My Power Back…………………………………..175

Prayers for Addicts………………………………..176

Recover Now………………………………………..…...179

Faith For You………………………………………....…180

Darkness I Invite You In To The Light………………......181

Heal My Harmful Patterns...182

Living in The Truth..183

Prayers for Mediums..184

Clear Me Now Jesus!..185

Prayer for Control Over Your Physical Body...............187

Gentle Reminder Prayer..189

3 Step Rebirthing & Balancing..................................191

Herbs for Clearing..192

Crystals for Clearing...198

Rules for Dowsing with A Pendulum...............................205

Permissions and Boundaries Over Your Body.......................208

After the Exorcism..210

Epilogue..214

About the Author..217

Foreword

I never understood any of this–and yet somehow, I found the way through the prayers that continued to come forward–I found the way to grasp some understanding of God. Working as a Healer and Psychic Medium I encountered many who were sick–physical sick, emotionally sick, mentally sick–but most often who I encountered were the spiritually sick. I came to understand malevolent energies exist–and anyone suffering from them can be healed.

Having been raised by Catholic parents, I spent many years learning and understanding the doctrine of the Catholic religion. My awakening started when I was 10 years old after seeing a television show on how to cure cancer. I watched the show and meditated as directed, only I didn't stop meditating and developed a deep love of the Spiritual life.

In my 20's while pregnant with my fourth child, after being advised by my Doctor to abort the baby because a test showed he 'had a hole in him' (they said, stomach, heart, or back) an Angel visited me and said my baby would be born healthy. Soon after the visit from the Angel, a high-tech ultrasound showed there was no hole, and the baby was healthy. I endured months of agony, and tearful days before the Angel came and brought peace into my life–in that moment I had total faith I would carry my unborn child to term and that he would be healthy. He was born healthy and beautiful–perfect in every way a baby should be.

In my 30's I had a dream about a boy who was murdered. Within months of the dream I learned the dream was real–and was shocked when a Psychic whose classes I had attended called me one morning and said, 'that dream you had–his family is on the phone'. With hesitation, I joined her on a visit to meet the boy's family.

The dreams did not stop….

I was able to offer information from the dreams to the detectives who worked on the case, and later offer some piece of mind to the retiring detective who worked for years to find the answers and bring peace to the family. That boy continues to be a cold case—but not to me, he visits me now as I work on cases, and he resides in Heaven. His Spirit is at peace.

I went on to provide information from the dreams and visions that continued to come. I have read for several cases, families of missing persons, the Police, and occasionally detectives who wander into my office anonymously. I have assisted Search and Rescue, Private Investigators, and I have assisted with various unsolved mysteries. I also help when dogs and cats go missing, as I am able.

I came to understand my gifts, and through many Spiritual explorations I came to understand to get out of my own way and let God help others through me. I have come to understand it is about peace.

In the year 2009 I was asked to read a haunted house. In the shower the morning I was to go to the house I was stunned to 'hear' through clairaudience the Latin Exorcism Rites being spoken to me by my Great Uncle Father Joe Donovan, a Jesuit Catholic Priest who resides in Heaven. Father Joe was my greatest Spiritual advisor as a child, next to my Father and my Mother. He passed away from cancer when I was a teenager–after admitting himself to the Swedish Hospital and allowing himself to be studied on the effects of dying through prayer and without medication.

During readings and healing sessions with clients my Uncle as well as Angels, Priests, Medicine Men and Women and other Benevolent Healers will come into my awareness and I become aware they are performing healing for the client. I have come to understand I need only open the door for the Highest Light to come through for the healing that is needed, and that it only happens when the client is ready to receive it. As I am holding the space for healing they also give instructions on what I am to do…. hold the clients hand, offer a kind word, pray a certain prayer, etc.

In 2014, I began having visions that led me to working with 'The Healing Team' the Ascended Masters who are what I call "The Doctors and Healers of the Universe". The team includes Master Jesus, Archangel Michael, Archangel Gabriel, "Dr. Ben", and many others totaling 15 altogether. I receive assistance from many benevolent ones on this side and the other as well. I cannot describe it–they 'come through' when a person needs healing. I must also at this time say thank you to Black Elk who comes through for healing those who resonate with Shamanic Healing as well.

Dr. Usui and Dr. Emoto I am blessed to receive their assistance through visions and during meditations. On occasion, I will receive messages from St Paul, St. Barnabas, and other Saints for others. As well as many Ascended Masters, and Master Buddha. It is very humbling, and I do my best to stay practical.

While running a healing arts center in Tacoma, Washington I was put to task to help people who were experiencing possessions. I had first encountered this in

2010 and had been helping to 'clear' people of 'other people's energies' back then, and came to understand that there are different levels of clearing – and each individual case is unique.

I learned that each person's healing was exclusive to their very belief system, their history, the type of trauma they may have incurred, past life history—as well as their current physical, mental, emotional, and most importantly, spiritual well-being.

I began to understand how to unravel what was dormant inside of them for the purpose of drawing it out for healing. I understood that anger and rage and emotions buried within could, in worse case, give home to entities. I came to understand the prayers that had been given to me through meditations years ago to heal someone of their repressed emotions were incredibly powerful healing prayers and that our emotional well-being is the key to sanity.

I don't remember the first exorcism I ever did, because there have been so many and Spirit has given me some sort of Spiritual amnesia so that I can remember the person and the situation, however when the Divine is in the process of healing others through me I do not remember many of the details that occur. I remember the before and the after very well. What I do know is that I stopped expecting my work to be normal. At one point I was performing 3 exorcisms a week, and currently I have helped with over 5 in the last two weeks. The prayers keep coming, and the people keep showing up. I began giving the prayers out to other healers who come to me saying they are also having the same phenomenon of people coming to them for this sort of help – spiritual cleansing.

Through the work, and through the prayers I came to understand that all darkness eventually fades to light. I understood the dying process, and the afterlife as it has been shown to me. I came to know our earth is sick with demons that exist on and inside of her – my guess is that for thousands of years we have been sending them to 'hell' (or inner earth) and in fact Spirit has shown me we need to send them to Heaven. I used to think that was unbelievable. Then I came to understand God's Mercy is unfathomable, that God's LOVE is ever reachable, that all creatures came from and eventually return to God.

I began to realize that everything EVERYTHING and every circumstance and situation has a purpose—even demonic possession.

I began to experience a personal miracle of faith in my life—and my faith was strengthened 10 million times by the Power of God. Fear has no place at all anymore—except fear of not remaining in faith, fear of not doing God's work, and fear of not hearing God's word. Those of us who are called to this work are disciples of those very principles—no matter your religion or spiritual background the principles apply to all who walk this path. I have come to accept my human nature—and understand that we are pitiful creatures born from the light into darkness—and as we come through the darkness back into the light—we can fully experience life.

For some they need a little help to step fully into the light, and so this little book of prayers comes forth to help anyone who needs healing and clearing and for any Spiritual Healers called by God to do this work. I pray this book protects you, helps you, and keeps your soul clear eternally–as well as all those who come to you for help. For anyone struggling to find the light, I hope this book helps you find it more easily, and once you've found it–have Faith in it. There is nothing greater than the Power of GOD's Love–which sets all Souls free.

This book is a little bit about my life and experiences, it is about the work, it is about the gift of God's grace, and it is a lot about the miracle of prayer.

I hope you use this book as a tool to assist you in staying and remaining clear, as a reference point for prayers that work, and for spiritual guidance. I have added healing techniques as well as information about different herbs and crystals that aid in healing and clearing.

In the event that you or someone you know are experiencing a haunting or possession or in need of healing / clearing work it is advised to consult with a professional Spiritual Warrior (never let ego interfere with true healing.... if you are not experienced—seek someone who is!) in addition to using the prayers, healing, and protection suggestions in this book.

Becoming from The Light

$\mathscr{I}$n the early morning, I went out for a walk. There was still snow on the ground. It was January 2016. As I gazed through my fogged glasses and felt the cold brisk wind on my cheeks my mind cleared. I walked and walked, and walked paying no mind to the distance or the cold. Inside, I had found peace and I was warm. I did not know where to begin, I did not know what had come to an end, I only knew where I was - somewhere I had not been for a while – free.

"It came back to me with a mighty wind"

Months before I had endured the dark night of the soul. I went through chaos–chaos I now have a name for. I had endured terrible pain, loss, and despair as I witnessed sickness around me, weakness around me, and darkness attempting to invade my life. I nearly lost my faith. It came back to me with a mighty wind.

Upon my return from a walk that morning, I experienced a total breakthrough. I knew I had released my attachments that had kept me from fully experiencing The Light. As I experienced the return of The Light, I wrote this Divine message that came in the form of a poem:

When we become the light -

we reflect on when we have not been the light

and can see all that is not light.

And when we become light,

a transformation begins

when we *remember.*

All that does not hold light fades,

and all that wants more light *follows.*

Truth is light.

Unconditional love is light.

In my breakthrough, I experienced the full rush and joy of the return of Light. I finally understood where I had held myself from fully experiencing The Light—because of my attachments and desires to relationships with people who would not release their attachments to darkness. I had finally let go.

Each one of us endures what is necessary for our individual awakening, and to some degree there may be suffering involved. In the case of my own despair, I was suffering a demonic attack that led me to truths and teachings so valuable—it can never be taken away. That truth is God. I unknowingly was receiving the answers for others through my own experience.

Prior to this experience I would have told you my faith was unbreakable, unshakable, and there wasn't any spiritual work I was not about to take on. I have worked as a healer now for 10 years. I really thought what I had seen happen to others could not happen to me. Until it did.

Today, my life is much different. I know that my Faith is so important that I must work to strengthen it daily. I put love and light into my Faith and spiritual practice daily and pray that it continues to strengthen. I am a powerful warrior for God and I will never take it for granted again.

"The deep wounds within me opened from this experience were given a chance to deeply and completely heal."

In my own personal experience, I saw firsthand a wave of destruction—and it was like a dark cloud that rolled in and would not release until all who were affected changed somehow and released it—or I released both them and it from my life. The darkness started in my community, and came into my life through whatever leaks it could come through. It affected people around me, then infected myself and those closest to me. I worked with numerous Shaman and Spiritual people, learned stronger purification rituals and tools, and learned to trust God and myself at an even deeper level—and most importantly how to ask for help, and who best to receive it from. Ultimately, I learned how to keep myself clear.

I discovered the deep wounds within me that opened from this experience were given a chance to deeply and completely heal.

I learned how to maintain a Godly vibration in the midst of tyranny, how to maintain clarity in my family, home, business, and relationships. I witnessed firsthand a forest fire almost take out my daughter's home when the chaos was at its worst. And I learned how to get rid of the chaos, and what was really causing it. Although it affected me and the lives of countless people around me, as the storm cleared the blessings started pouring in–the lessons began making sense, and God's hand in it all seemed obvious even in my clairvoyance I was blocked from seeing the blessings as the destruction was happening. When the darkness cleared, the wisdom sank in. You might not believe it unless you were there to experience it first hand or have experienced something like it yourself. In fact, you might not believe what I have to say at all—but I've learned that is not my business. This book is not for believers. This book is for everyone. Where I once could see The Light—I now can see the dark, because I come FROM THE LIGHT. When you can see it, with God's help-*you can clear it.*

In this book, I have included Latin translations for certain prayers. My father studied to be a Jesuit Catholic Priest and dropped out of the seminary just months before his ordination—and soon after met my mother. Growing up my Father always told me the Latin version of the English words I was learning. Even in the months before his passing away, in his 80's, he still spoke the translations on occasion. The Latin language is not a second language to me; however, it is a familiar language. The Latin words are considered 'permanent' or fixed and unchangeable—that is why I have included these translations. The words are truth, fixed, and connected to God's word.

Because I am Multi-Denominational Ordained Minister I have included various teachings and prayers that come from Spirit.

The Holy Bible is a sacred tool that was channeled by many prophets and includes valuable teachings of Jesus Christ. It should be used both as a reference and a guide. Although some of the teachings are out of date (or hard to understand) it continues to offer valuable information and help, and serve as a primary reference of truth and protection for both Spiritual Warriors, and all people.

The Christ Ray (also referred to as Light Ray) is the energy body of the Holy Spirit that contains Master Jesus, the Holy Disciples, the Archangels, God's Army of Angels, and Ascended Masters that protect the Souls of mankind, and help mankind to ascend. I refer to the Christ Ray in prayers and reference it in the writings here.

I have included Catholic, Christian, Pagan (pre-Christian) and Native American terms in these prayers. I am respectful of all benevolent religions, and these prayers will work for you no matter who you are or what religious or spiritual background you come from. Because I am a Medium I love and respect all paths that are from, hold to, and lead to God. I do not have the luxury of not seeing—because I see, feel, and hear the benevolent there is no choosing a particular sect or religion so I practice the old ways—of listening to Spirit, and walking on the Blue Road in a Red Road World. I follow the Spiritual teachings of Jesus, and practice listening to the wind.

While writing this book Angels came to me many times and offered assistance, hope, and brought prayers to me to write. I was visited twice by a Goddess who calls herself The Blue Crystal Goddess. I saw her in a vision—she is wrapped in Archangel Michael's wings—and comes to clear those who do his work. I felt a powerful surge or energetic clearing and felt profound healing from her visits. I feel she will always be with me.

Some would say–why write about exorcisms? A friend helped me to understand that I am writing about what I know.

Anyone who is practicing the Spiritual work of Jesus will benefit from these prayers. Only God chooses who performs healing and exorcisms. So, there is no fear in publishing these works here. Those who are called to this work will benefit from it. Those who need clearing will benefit from it.

"Be safe, be mindful what you let into your house"

A very important rule to remember–if you clear someone else clear yourself thoroughly–don't bring it home. No matter what level of malevolence, unclean Spirits and unclean energetics will happily cling to you, anyone you know, and anything in your home–without prejudice. Wise people do what is necessary to maintain safety and a happy home. Foolish people ignore good advice. Be safe, be mindful what you let into your house....your life, your mind, your business, and your physical body. Never let your guard down, increase your knowing that you are protected by God, and take actions daily to connect to your benevolent protectors and thank them.

Nearly a year after channeled that poem (pg. 26) after that clear wintry walk–it all makes sense. **God** *has a master plan.* Everything happens for a reason.

Hauntings, clearings, possessions and wrestling with deep internal and external demons are a part of Spiritual awakening–for some. The deep internal and often past life clearings and current life challenges that occur are experienced to teach us, heal us, transform us, and ultimately clear us of a path that does not and/or did not serve us–and raise our will to the alignment of God's will for us…which is ultimately our true purpose.

Curses from past lives and biblical times, if not broken and healed can carry forward. Unhealthy ties and addictions that bind a person from a past life or past time in this life or ancestry can affect a person in this life in the now if the root cause that allowed it in the first place is not healed. Trauma's from this life or an unhealed past life, traumatic death or life, or disbelief in God, or feelings of unworthiness can manifest a root belief or emotion that lays the ground work for malevolent darkness to enter. Much of the healing work that pastors, ministers, priests, and medicine people do is to help clear the roots of disease and help a suffering soul to raise the awareness of where the unhealthy root is actively manifesting itself in a person's mental beliefs and thoughts, spiritual ignorance or blockage, physical sickness or fatigue and depression, and emotional burdens. When the awareness of the root cause that allowed malevolence (in whatever form) to bind and have power over a person (body, mind, will, soul) is discovered—once it is spoken that it no longer has power, and God is restored in that person— it is the Universal Law that malevolence must release, and then has no power to remain. When this happens—true healing can **and does** occur.

Malevolent darkness in whatever form serves to cloud the Soul's purpose, forces us to look at what remains to be healed, and gives us a newfound awareness that the will is SACRED. When a person heals, takes back their power, and claims their will is God's will and claims their right to a joyful happy life – they become a fearless warrior for God and an example to all others suffering.

Bring God into your heart and God will be in your house, your life, your relationships, and your work.

Becoming From The Light – the Soul experiences freedom, the Soul experiences exhilaration, the Soul experiences once more. Without The Light – the Soul is trapped, be it by the mind, or by the past, or by the darkness.

When one is truly free–in The Light, one experiences, and is free to experience the meaning, the truth, the innocence, the humility, and the wisdom of God. Then, one is truly free to experience the Divine within oneself.

That Light, as it has always been, and as it is now, is free.

God's Light

The Holy Spirit moves in the world, and is in all things. God's Light does not 'come' it IS already present. God, Great Spirit, Allah, Universe, or however you shall say the Highest Benevolent Source of Power that has given us Creation and is our Creator—is already there, and always available.

Through the power of your mind and your connection to God—that is 'your' awareness—you can infuse God's Light into your body, mind, and Spirit.

Through the power of your faith and positive intentions you can increase God's Healing Light into: your life, your family, your water, your body, your land, land, your circumstances, your community, your next doctor's appointment, your education, and your relationships, etc. The Power of God is unlimited. Only our awareness of God is limited. How God works in our lives is unlimited. Only our awareness of God working in our lives is limited.

Infusing God's Light into your life takes practice. Daily practice. When you find that yourself or someone near you is experiencing spiritual sickness, be mindful that there is a block of God's Light in or around your life. If it is someone you know, be careful not to allow their block to limit The Light in your own life. Staying positive in the midst of others who are struggling may take some practice, in this case all you can do is strengthen yourself, pray for them and say clearing prayers. It may take time to get back on track and release the block (or it may happen instantly and miraculously right now!). Stay faithful, and hopeful.

Often a spiritual sickness occurs when a people have fallen off his/her path—the path he/she came here to take. God wants to work in your life—it is up to you to say yes. When you move farther and farther away from God, spiritual sickness occurs—because your Soul is connected to God—you are connected to God and the more you move away from

God the farther away you become from yourself. Have you ever heard someone say, "I feel like I'm losing myself"?

When someone feels blocked they often feel a sense of sadness. Sadness is not experiencing joy. Joy happens when we are connected to self–our true nature and true calling. We can become blocked in life from so many things –job loss, loss of a loved one, feeling hopeless, feeling victimized, overcoming trauma. Blocks can allow our awareness to be so decreased that we begin functioning less than our Soul's potential and when we function less than our Soul's potential for any extended period of time we begin to adjust to it, and over time accept it as our reality–turning to lower vibrational or depressed behaviors such as addiction, promiscuity, criminal behavior (minor or major), and ultimately begin feeling we are lying to our self. All blocks can be removed. Imagine building an Egyptian pyramid–it was built one stone at a time. God wants to start magically moving stones in your life and build an amazing temple out of you.

You can start out by simply asking God for what is needed in your life and asking God to remove the blocks to receiving joy now.

Experiencing God's Light in your life is like taking a walk on a new pathway, one more magical that you have experienced ever before—things just seem to make better sense, what you need you find more easily, happiness is present not distant, and life has more meaning.

What is a Haunting?

A haunting is a symptom of a sickness.
You who are haunted can be healed.

You can be haunted in your home, your mind, your relationships, your career, your life. You who are haunted are haunted by the past. It is the past alone or anyone living in the past (alive or deceased) that is haunting you. To become healed from any form of haunting you must start truly living in the now and release what is keeping you from your light and your life.

In addition, items can be haunted, including homes, land, jewelry, etc –anything with an energetic attachment or 'energetic mark' on it from someone who is or was toxic and who 'possessed' the item (including home, land, jewelry, etc.) that person being living or deceased, however usually deceased and not crossed into Heaven.

On occasion an item can be so 'haunted'—or marked with negative possessive energy, that it must be neutralized in some way (vinegar, bury it in the earth 7 days, salt, soaked in water, etc.) or burned.

The highest and best is to cross over to Heaven All Souls trapped on the earth plane, especially any trapped Soul that is causing negative possessive energy—for that is the root cause, unless the person is living—in which case Spiritual Healing is the key to clearing, and even then, items from before the person cleared should be neutralized, burned, or discarded if they continue to be haunted or remain discordant.

We don't and should never have burned Witches. A Witch (or Warlock) is a woman or man who stands in his or her Power *and in* The Light, usually with Pre-Christian, Shamanic, and/or Pagan beliefs. All Witches go to Heaven, and they are the Healers and Herbalists and Medicine Men and Women in your community. In the old days, those who worked to heal haunted people and things were the very ones accused of causing it.

God chooses the Healers and Medicine Men and Women—just as God chooses the Teachers, Farmers, Lawyers, and Musicians. It is a calling, and years ago, if you were called and you were listening to your own guidance as a Healer, it was frowned upon.

My mother taught me—we fear what we do not know. On occasion a person (from any culture/religion-including Witches and Pastors) can become possessed with dark energy and power hungry and not 'Of the Light'. We must use our discernment at all times and be cautious. Listening to God is considered using the highest discernment. Anyone can develop stronger discernment through the regular practice of daily meditation and regular Spiritual Practices to develop the ears to hear God. In Hindu, daily practice is called Puja. Through Yoga, Reiki, meditation, and the clearing techniques in this book—you will also learn to clear karmic blockages and allow for greater discernment of God's will.

The sanest people can become possessed if there is a 'leak in them' where darkness can get through (ego, hurt, unfaithfulness, pride, depression, etc.). That is why as Pastors, Priests, Nuns, Ministers, High Priests, High Priestesses, and Spiritual Advisors, we have a duty to ourselves and those who come to us for help to maintain our own Spiritual Fitness. They need healing, not punishment they need God.

Signs and Symptoms of a Haunting

~ House or Person ~

Bad/Rancid Smells (usually in one spot in the home like a hallway, or corner) *where there is no cat box present*

The People in the Home Argue

Keeping the Lights Dimly Lit

Not Letting Light into the House

You feel bad when you are there

Bed Wetting

Unexplainable Sounds

Unexplainable Activity

The Sound of Footsteps

The Sounds of Cupboards/Doors Opening or Closing when no one is there

Things being out of place, or being moved when you're not looking, or when you're looking

Extreme Rage, Anger, Violence

Drug Abuse, Alcoholism

Seeing Shadows in the House

Dogs barking at nothing

Cats arguing/agitated/excessive peeing

A feeling that you can't leave

Depression while you are there, and feeling better when you are not

Candles won't stay lit

Sage won't stay lit

Music skips/changes the channel/turns off

Computers 'doing their own thing'

Computers won't work right

TV skips/changes the channel/turns on and off

TV, seems to be only shows of a dark nature/demonic

Unexplainable smell of smoke or alcohol

A bad feeling when you enter one area of the house or one room in the house

The feeling that you're being watched

Fear of going to sleep

Seeing Ghosts in the House

Smudging the House and Yourself and it helps for a while but does not go away

Getting angry for no reason

Feeling poor health/unhealthy since you moved in

Nightmares

Unusual alarms going off (car alarms, etc.)

Paranoia that is 'uncommon to you' (never felt this way before)

Relationships Falling Apart 'since you moved in' as if 'something is coming between you'

Feeling you have memory loss (losing things, things not where they should be)

People don't want to come over/in

The air 'feels heavy'

The Children are not themselves

Spiritual People coming into your life and it seems 'out of place' (coming to help you)

Unexplained Fear

A knowing that 'something is going on'

Lights flickering / going on and off

Cars acting up/won't start/stall

Help seems 'prevented from getting there'
Calls being 'lost'

Hearing voices on a recorder, or on your phone that 'don't belong there' and are unexplainable

Seeing Ghosts / Spirits in your photos

Having dead worms come to your door

Infestations of pests: lice, fleas, flies

An overall feeling of 'being pushed out'

Unexplained Physical Sickness
(that usually lasts weeks or months).

Anxiety when you are in the home

*note, these are possible signs and symptoms based on what I have seen and from what clients have experienced and told me through the years. It is not all inclusive, and may or may not be caused by a malevolent Spirit.

I am not a Doctor and these signs and symptoms of haunting and possession are for the purpose of healing a haunting, or a person experiencing a haunting or a possession and are not a medical diagnosis (or to be used as such) or to be used in place of any medical treatment. For any medical emergency call 911. For any physical sickness call a Doctor.

For a haunting or a possession – call God.

Then call a Spiritual Warrior.

The Process of Going to Heaven

Not all Spirits are malevolent, (harmful) and may in fact be your dearest friend or loved one who has not crossed into Heaven, or not 'all the way' to Heaven.

I have witnessed many heartwarming moments working as a Medium for others. Working as a Medium, I am able to receive messages from loved ones who have passed away, and then translating those messages to the living and often grieving family here. Most often Spirits come through to offer love and support. Messages let the family know they are not alone, and often give a sense of peace. When a deceased loved one comes through that has not crossed over into Heaven, it is a gift to assist the living family in helping their loved one take that step to cross into the Light.

Through years of working with clients and their loved ones who have passed away, I came to understand there is a process, and that process is unique to each individual and their needs. I have come to understand that when a person passes away they are either 'two feet here on earth', 'one foot in Heaven and one foot here on Earth' or 'Two feet in Heaven'.

Two feet here on earth means the deceased person is Earth Bound and has not yet crossed over into the Light. I believe that is what Hell is—being stuck on Earth after Death and not crossing over into Heaven. In the Catholic Religions that is referred to as Purgatory. When a person passes away from trauma, suicide, unexpectedly, with a criminal or violent background, mental instability, or has had no Spiritual belief system or believes there is no such things as God—or was raised without any Spirituality they may be 'two feet on Earth' after death until their Ancestors, Angels, God takes them to Heaven or a Spiritual worker crosses them. These are the Spirits who are most prone to 'possess' another person. Externally feeding on another person's light, aura, energy or internally—co-habitating in another person's body.

In some circumstances, the living and grieving person is so disturbed by the loss of the loved one–that they pull on the Spirit to stay, and can *unintentionally* alter the process, and delay their loved one from going to Heaven. In rare circumstances, *the living person* can possess their deceased loved one and not allow them to leave (until they realize what they are doing, begin their own healing process, or have spiritual assistance). I feel it is in a normal loving attempt to not abandon the living suffering loved ones, that sometimes a Spirit will forego Heaven for a time. In my experience when the suffering living person does finally let go–their loved ones often release to Heaven, and when this happens, the true healing begins for all those affected who are left behind, as well as the Spirit who transitions to Heaven on their journey.

One foot here on Earth and One Foot in Heaven
is the most common transitory state a Spirit enters after death. The Spirit passes into Heaven and then if necessary takes time to heal in the Healing Chamber (a place in Heaven), then their Spirit returns to Earth to help their loved

ones through the grief process. This is a very natural part of death, and lasts approximately one year.

Two feet in Heaven occurs when a person passes away and their Spirit goes Straight to Heaven, has done all their work here on Earth and for whatever reason is called to Stay in Heaven – they will 'visit' their loved ones on Earth, come through in dreams, bring them gifts, however they come 'flying in' as if from above –no longer tied to the Earth. This can happen right away, or when the time is right. Very Spiritual people in my experience go straight to Heaven. There is not much between them and God, therefore their ascension is much easier. In my experience their loved ones also have an easier time in the grief process.

I was not ready for my Mother to pass. Months before her sickness progressed a Psychic I know stopped me in a hallway at a Psychic Fair and told me that when the time comes, that it was my job to cross my Mother to Heaven. I was thankful for the message, but did not know what it meant.

When my mother Helen was hospitalized for a blockage (bile duct and intestines)–it became clear suddenly that she was getting ready to take her journey, yet we remained for a few days in hope. When the Doctors said she was not going to survive the surgery–that she was too weak to recover–our family was devastated by the news. After a middle of the night call from the nurse–only a few short days later I headed to the hospital to comfort my Mother and I remembered the words of the woman in the hall months before. When there were only minutes left–with my brother Mike by my side and my Father on the other side of the hospital bed I gathered my strength, and held my Mother's hand and closed my eyes and went into Spirit.

The Spirits of my Ancestors and Angels filled the room. The sounds of the monitors and my Mother's shallow breathing were silenced from my mind and become blocked from my knowing–I went into the void and all I could feel was her Spirit.

As I held her hand I was suddenly transported into a vision–as if the visions were coming straight from her touch.

I saw her as a little baby, then as a little girl with her Mother, visions of her childhood, I saw her riding her bicycle, the house where she grew up, her Father, I watched as a psychic movie screen that seemed to hang in front of me played vision after vision of my Mother's life–flashing one after another until the visions flashed by rapidly and then a voice said ' It is time' . I knew if I let go of her hand the visions would stop so I held tight and asked for strength to hang on and help her through this. My physical body remained corded to the earth and my Spirit floated out of my body as I went with her Spirit. As my Mother began to fade, I saw nothing but light and a soft sweet feeling came over me. I went like a sweet drift with her ....

Then with a shock I was back in the room, holding my Mother's lifeless hand, still and warm.

The monitors had been silenced and the room was still with my Fathers and my Brothers and my grief. The woman who gave me life–gave me the greatest gift–**to be with her as she watched the video of her life and see it**

with her and to witness her joy and her journey to Heaven. I don't know how long it lasted – minutes? But, the moment seemed to last for hours. To this day, I can still see it if I want to, and it fills me with peace. She saw the trials and she saw the joys, every puppy was there, and all the love…all the love…and all the love.

It is hard to understand how our loved ones come to us when and how we need them from Heaven–I only know that they do.

A few weeks after my Mother's death I was struggling with a bank employee at my parent's bank. I had a vision of her, it was the first vision I had since the day she passed. Only, in this vision she showed up riding a broom, she was dressed up like a witch (very NOT my mother but she has great humor and knew I'd think it was very funny which I did I've never forgotten it!) and with my psychic sight I saw her riding above that bank employee who suddenly had a change of heart and became very kind and obliging.

In reading for those who have recently passed, I have often seen visions of Spirits in a place I can only describe as a healing room. While there, it is my limited understanding that their Spirit receives healing and awareness as they adjust to Heaven and their Spirit – now a Heavenly Body. The room is very bright, with hues of translucent blue, with many Angels around – and I have also seen some sort of Psychic Surgery being performed in the room on a few spirits who died traumatically. Upon leaving the healing room that I call the Healing Chamber–they often return to loved ones on Earth to help them with their healing, or, they may go straight into the next body, or remain to experience Heaven.

I have seen this be one of the most trying times of the human spirit during the deep sorrow and sadness of losing someone close. I have experienced the grief of losing a close relative, as well as a close friend. After the loss of a loved one the devastation can last a long time, and can bring on depression.

I have seen husbands whose wives have passed (and vice versa) long to follow them to Heaven for being without them seems unbearable in the early days. With the support of family and faith—and a will to live, they do recover. For some the death of a loved one will bring up other sorrows from the past and re-open wounds.

Depending on the type of the loss, the devastation can last weeks to years—and can even be considered traumatic. This time of grief is a walk of Faith and Trust in God. It is part of our individual learning process and conscious awakening to understand the process of death is to also come to understand that we are always alive.

Somewhere in our grief process we finally find the strength to 'let go' and continue. *At that point, we can learn through the **physical disconnection** with our Loved One and the **Spiritual Re-connection** with them - and with God - that Heaven exists, and our loved ones are always with us.*

For anyone struggling with this now—I suggest let your grief work with you (as it was said to me a long time ago) and not against you—and when your ready trust God again and let go—give the pain to Jesus.

Allow the pain and sadness (anger, etc.) to emerge as you are able. For anyone suffering from grief; counseling, a routine Doctor Check-up, Reiki healing, Shamanic healing, help groups (especially suicide survivor groups for anyone who has lost a loved one to suicide), and self-help books on grief and loss, are recommended.

Through my experience and experience with clients I have come to understand that repressing emotions such as sadness, and anger from the grief caused by losing a loved one can cause physical manifestations (illness) within the body—[PTSD] sometimes years later. Therefore, taking special care to maintain your health and making choices that allow your grief and healing are very important after the loss of a loved one. As they do their healing, it is your time to heal as well.

Healing is a form of surrender, an acknowledgement of what has changed, and how life is different in some ways (or drastically) because of the change. Naturally, as life begins to reflect this new way of living, healing starts to occur. Crying, resting, meditation, spending time allowing emotions to come to the surface to be released are all a part of the healing process. Letting go of fear.

Everyone processes differently and there is no wrong way. Without taking control of your health and healing needs, untreated sadness from the loss of a loved one can manifest in the form of continued loss (job loss, etc.), and can negatively impact daily life, career, and relationships. I have had some say to me during their deepest times of depression that 'it feels as though they destroyed my life'–this is not the case, however without taking the time to heal, and acknowledge the deep hurt and pain associated to the loss, returning to the joys of life are delayed. Some perceive the need for deep healing as a sign of weakness, however emotions will find their way to the surface as a person is able to process them.

For some people healing from the loss of a loved one brings on a newfound Spirituality, connection to God, and enlightenment.

What is a Demon?

A demon is anything that is demonizing someone, something, or any group of people or community. I like to think of a demon as a plague, in other words it has plagued someone, something, or a group of people or community. A demon falls into three categories:

1) An Earth Bound Spirit that has not crossed into the Light usually *for many years* and has 'gained power' through feeding on living people's energy also known as a poltergeist (which may also refer to a group of Earth Bound Spirits not crossed into the Light for many years).

2) A fallen angel or group of fallen angels that are plaguing the Earth and Earth people. Everything eventually comes to Light, even fallen angels. When we fall, we do eventually heal, the same is true for Angels, and only God knows what to do with them so–if you encounter a demon of this nature pray also for the Light to come to this being. Love is the antidote, **unconditional love**–is the cure.

3) Earth Bound deceased or living malevolent alien Spirits. Earth bound alien Spirits are not 'of this earth' also referred to as 'not of this dimension' (in other words they did not originate here–their ancestors are not from here. Either they died during their travels here, died while they were here, or somehow ended up here. Some genuinely do not like humans

and will demonize them, they will do anything to continue feeding on human life force energy as it is all they have known possibly for hundreds of years. It might surprise you to know that even aliens go to heaven. Living alien Spirits (in the seen and unseen) ***who are harmful to humans*** are demons. There are alien beings (other worldly) who are wonderful and benevolent, both in the now and deceased who share our Universe.

Demons can be 'called' by accident or intention. The Ouija board's original intention was to conjure up Spirits. The Ouija board is a perfect example of ignorance, and I have personally cleared too many people to count who opened doors to malevolent energies while using a Ouija board.

Do not speak to demons. If you happen to know a demon's name, it is wise to remember it, and only use it in the case you are banishing. Do not feed them any power.
In the past, I experienced a person who was not **aligned** with the Holy Spirit (God, the Ascended Masters, and the Universal *Benevolent* Light Ray) who called upon Spirits in

ritual magic, accident, ignorance, and plain old curiosity, and accidentally allowed in a demon. Using the power of prayer and positive intentions is **vital** when invoking assistance—make sure it is ALWAYS from the Light Realm. Make sure to set your intentions when in prayer and/or ritual that assistance if from God and *Benevolent* Guides, Angels, and Ascended Masters, etc.

"The demon may have been on earth in a miserable state for many years"

A demon may be attached to an object, a house, a person, an animal, a community, land, a mirror, a past life, a spouse, etc. Not all Earth Bound Spirits are demons. As I have mentioned some Spirits who are earth bound are our loved ones—and have issues to work through here on earth. Strong discernment is necessary in determining an Earth Bound Spirit from a demon, and the two are treated quite differently.

Someone with a demonic attachment (either internally or externally) will need *multiple levels of clearing*—and as the demon may have been on earth in a miserable state for many years, so may have the person with the attachment. In my experience the type of person experiencing a demonic attachment is someone who has experienced long periods of depression, addiction, or an unhappy state of being for many years (sometimes hidden from peers). Like attracts like—a person who is lacking peace and is feeding on negativity may inadvertently leave themselves open to this type of attachment. I know one person who was possessed for over 14 years, and another person who was possessed for over 10 years. It is through the power of God that a person clears, and no matter how long a person has been afflicted, clearing can happen NOW.

Serious attention to positive beautiful Spiritual Light Filled vibrations of unconditional Love and Light surrounding any situation or person who is or was previously infected with any form of demonic energetic is needed immediately. Stop the darkness. Give it no power to exist and cause harm in your life. Let the Light flow in, through powerful prayers and intentions, and personal protection and projections of Light.

A strong will to live, and a strong sense of God–leaves a demon with no place to nest.

God's Angels, Thank you for your protection from Malevolent Spirits

What is a Possession?

Any form that has Power over your Soul. Until you give your Soul back to God, from where it originally came, you are open for malevolent possession. You can give your Soul to God by turning the Power over to God, by trusting and walking a path of Faith and by saying out loud "I give my soul to God". This is the ultimate trust, and it is the ultimate 'knowing' you already know in your heart this is what saves Souls—to return if you ever left. Some return easily, some never left, and some take the hard road.

I don't know what you're healing from that led you who took the hard road here…maybe it was abuse, low self-esteem, death of a loved one that left you vulnerable in your time of grief, a family history of allowing negative energy to have power and control over your life-or the lives of those you love, drug abuse, a continuous hostile environment, alcoholism, hopelessness, imprisonment, shame, or fear.

"An attitude of disappointment that nothing can fill the void"

Unhealthy attitudes can also possess a person, or allow a possession to intrude. These attitudes may include but are not limited to: an attitude of disappointment, intolerance, judgment, ignorance, distrust, being a victim, giving focus on perverse ideas and thoughts, power hunger, hate, immoral grandiosity, ego, isolation, racism, sexism, disdain, and despair.

Of these, an attitude of disappointment is most common that can leave a person open to a malevolent possession. An attitude of disappointment that nothing can fill the void—the person with this attitude may try to fill 'the void' with drugs, alcohol, poor relationships, or a focus on more of what feels like disappointment. What fills the void is God. Filling the void with anything that is unhealthy for you gives power away. Pray to have an attitude of a prayerful heart, right achievement, joy, sanity, and love.

—Whatever the cause of the possession the treatment is simple—the cure is GOD.

Two Forms of Possession

There are two forms of Possession:
Internal and External

The two forms of possession that I have experienced are internal and external. That being said, it is exactly what it sounds like—either an energy is in your aura and 'trying to possess you' and is negatively impacting your life—or it is internal—literally another person's Spirit or an Entity had entered into yours and is physically co-habitating in your body. A Body can be occupied by more than one Spirit, but only if the owner of the body allows it, or gives permission for it to happen either accidentally or intentionally.

An external possession is the most common type of possession. The prayers in this book are designed to help prevent either type of possession from occurring.

The 4 Most Common Reasons

Although an internal possession is fairly uncommon, and usually an external possession is more likely, unfortunately, it does happen.

In my experience, beginning Mediums who don't know about setting boundaries, a person using hard drugs or addicted to prescription drugs, someone who is in deep mourning over a lost loved one, or someone who is angry with God (for various reasons) in my experience are the 4 most common reasons for an internal possession to occur.

It is very important for Mediums no matter what your skill level–to understand how to clear yourself and to know how to set boundaries within the Spirit World. I would even go so far as to say if you don't believe it can happen to you– you are in danger of it happening and should ask God to protect you from possessions of any kind. I would go even farther to say–anyone who is 'playing' is in a danger zone. If it is not your 'calling' to work with your gifts in the capacity of a Medium working for others then please stop dabbling now before you or someone else gets hurt. All Mediums, no matter skill level or calling, need to stay clear of drugs and alcohol, and learn clearing techniques. It takes a special person to do this type of work, and a little commitment goes a long way.

A person addicted to drugs and/or alcohol may be experiencing an ill will, inability to set boundaries, and lacking the independent thought (free of chemical influence) that is necessary to clear oneself, and stay clear. That is why I have dedicated a portion of this book to prayers for addicts. In my experience addiction and possession go hand in hand.

For anyone in deep mourning over the loss of a loved one, or for anyone who is angry with God, healing is the course of action. Let the healing start now.

Signs and Symptoms of an External Possession

It comes and goes, is not constant

Unexplained Headaches

Feeling Nauseated

Feel something 'hovering' around you, especially at night or wake up feeling this way

Irritable or Argumentative for no apparent reason that can't be justified by any physical health issues

You don't care anymore, feel burdened by negativity.

You don't want to do anything

Personality changes, aren't interested in your usual things

Don't feel you have 'the energy'

Feel attacked

Bad hygiene

Rotting Teeth / Teeth Falling Out / Cavities

Avoid getting out of bed or out of the house

Most likely experiencing some of the signs and symptoms of a haunting as well

Unusual feelings of depression not characteristic of your true nature (doesn't seem to make any sense-no reason to be depressed-and you don't care)

Signs and Symptoms of an Internal Possession

Others ask you why you're not yourself and you do not feel like yourself (unexplainable)

Migraines

Alienating yourself

Blurry/blurred vision/eyes look blurred

Feeling sick 'all the time'

Posture is not usual

Extreme Rage, Anger, Violence

Drug Abuse, Alcoholism

Seething Hate

Seeing Spirits / Hearing Voices but don't seem to realize that it's "not normal" (unable to discern messages from benevolent Guides and Angels from Earth Bound Spirits or malevolent entities that are haunting you or your home – being unable to discern "the good from the bad")

Acting irrational

Making unusually poor or strange choices

You don't care anymore about anything you once cared about and others notice

Personality changes, aren't interested in your usual things

Sexual promiscuity / womanizing / cheating / porn / acting out sexually

Compulsive behavior not usual to you

Have energy, however it is 'unusual' you and you don't 'seem like yourself'

Appear 'split personality' to others who know you and know you have never been diagnosed with any mental condition

Want to hurt others who get in your way

Are always right—unable to reason or listen to anyone

Bad hygiene / smelling strange or bad

Bed Wetting / Loss of Bladder or Bowel Control

Rotting Teeth / Teeth Falling Out / Cavities

Avoid getting out of bed or out of the house

Unexplainable Sounds

Unusually active during times when you normally would not be active

Talking about demons, the devil, dark things

Saying weird perverse things you normally would not say

You 'smite' God, make negative comments about God, religion, other's beliefs, laugh at them, spit on them, make grimacing faces, stick out your tongue.

Memory Loss

Animals act very strange around you, won't come near you.

Dismissing Nightmares or Strange things as 'nothing'

Lights flicker when you're in the room

Most likely the people around you are feeling they need to avoid you but may not understand why.

Others hear voices coming from you that
are not your own or "don't sound like you"

*Some symptoms of internal and external possession are similar; however
the internal symptoms are more intense.*

All Cords Must be Cut

The cords must be cut—the cords to all things, people (living and deceased), places, and objects that are sick and toxic need to be released from your life, in order for you to heal.

The cords from you as well as your mother's side and father's side to any demonic subjugation, and malevolent entities/energies all the way back to Adam and Eve (or even before if necessary) need to be cut and severed from you.

All cords to toxic people, emotions, and beliefs and behaviors that are malevolent/harmful need to be cut and a healing needs to occur.

Cutting the cords does not always mean leaving those you love—it does however always mean leaving the chaos and returning to a life of sanity. In some cases, it means starting all over.

Most insanity is the work of malevolence,

- Chaos is its name.

Boundaries Need to Be Set In Place

I came to understand through Spirit, and through years of experience that my gift as a Medium is a gift that is very special and must be carefully protected.

Without the proper protection and the understanding of what it truly means to be a Medium—one should not endeavor to work with a gift of this nature or you become in danger of possession.

Many of the people who have come to me for clearing, healing, and help are spiritual people. Of these, many are Mediums.

I have also had to reach out for help. In my early 20's I decided to take a 'break' from God. Soon after the death of a beautiful friend whose life was shortened by addiction and tragedy—I found myself in a dark hole, a pit of depression, haunted—and *it lasted for several years*.

I remember the day I 'woke up' and announced I was going back to church. Although it didn't last long back at the Catholic Church—I never left God.

I was destined to discover a Spiritual Path that would lead me to be the Multi-Denominational Ordained Minister I am today. I went on to discover several Spiritual Pathways, met many teachers, and learned many ways to experience, worship, and cherish God.

Once you encounter a personal haunting of this nature—it is a lesson you never forget, and staying clear and maintaining spirituality naturally becomes a way of life.

Not having proper boundaries with the living as well as the deceased (earth-bound) is the primary reason spiritual people experience being possessed.

People who are angry with God, 'smiting God', and rebelling against God are prime targets, as their walls are down and they are spiritually unprotected.

Boundaries are often taught to us by our parents, teachers, Spiritual Teachers, and social upbringing.
It isn't hard to figure out how good your boundaries are or are not–look at your parents, siblings, your current relationships, your children, etc.–do they have good boundaries? If the answer is no–the chances that you need to strengthen yours are likely. If you feel you need to strengthen your boundaries–then you do. If you feel you do not need to strengthen your boundaries–but everyone around you considers you a pushover–then you do.

What is an Exorcism?

It is releasing a malevolent entity or entities
that are attached to a person, place, or thing–usually a person.
These days we call them 'clearings' more often than not–
however the correct term for releasing a malevolent energy,
entity, demon, fallen angel, alien, or earth bound trapped
Spirit from a person is Exorcism.

Sometimes while giving a Reiki Healing Session a
clearing will occur spontaneously. Because I am a Medium,
Spirits who are ready to cross to Heaven (and some who are
just curious or who want to be heard) come to me for help
and understanding. Jesus, and other Ascended Masters and
teachers assist in the clearing process, as well as Archangel
Michael. It is a gift to be able to offer this kind of assistance,
and whenever possible, if family is present, I guide them,
through my connection–to help their Loved Ones go to
Heaven. An Exorcism is however, a more in–depth process
than an aura clearing.

In one case in 2014 I remember a woman who had the Spirit of a man killed while at war, trapped in her. He did not want to leave either his men, or his family. The woman had been on anti-depressants for years and was drained of all her energy and most of her life force by the time she came into my office. He was a friend of someone she knew.

I determined he had been there for about 5 years. The woman was sad and lonely, and also a medium who had never learned how to work with her gifts, and instead had shut them off. She was hearing voices, and said she had 'gone crazy' and even her medication was not helping. The clearing lasted several hours, and because she was under the influence of medication I was careful to stay within the realms of what she could handle at the time. She came back for a second clearing, and was still experiencing some of her symptoms but to a lesser degree. I performed a full exorcism. The man who had been with her finally came out, and all his rage and pain released from the woman. He crossed over to Heaven, and she left my office as if nothing had happened. His presence within her had been blocking her memory, and once he left she appeared calm, clear, and like an entirely different person. I gave her some teachings on tuning into her gifts, and she drove off.

In another case, I went to a haunted house, by request, to investigate what was going on. When I got there, not only was the house haunted, but two members of the family were addicted to meth, the mother was a psychic who had not honed her gifts and was 'unsure about God'. The husband of the woman who called me out to the house was severely possessed by malevolent Spirits–and was an intuitive man himself. I performed a clearing on the house. However not much changed, so I performed an exorcism on the man, at which point not only did the man clear, but the house cleared. It was as if the Spirits attached to the man were keeping the Spirits in the house as well. I received an update, the husband and wife moved out on their own and were doing fine.

In another case, I went to investigate a haunting and discovered the Spirit of a man, through psychic sight, who had killed himself in the garage was still in the home of the couple who called me out. The husband and man of the house was having a really hard time in life–feeling he couldn't advance in his career, feeling depressed, didn't want to leave the house. The Spirit of the man who was deceased and Earth Bound had externally attached himself to the man of the house. The man of the house thought the deceased man's thoughts were his own, and he became depressed. I did a house clearing, a clearing for the husband and wife, and compassionately spoke to the deceased man until he stepped into the light–and went to Heaven with the help and encouragement of the husband and wife.

Things got back on track for them.

My favorite case is the story of a very gifted but very haunted young Alaskan Native woman. Her husband drove her to my office one day many years ago for an exorcism. He knew exactly what she needed. I was a little off guard and took my time to assess the woman. She was on anti-depressants, and was having physical symptoms that were unexplainable to Doctors. She feared she was going to die, and said she trusted no Psychics (she had had a previous negative experience with someone). Her haunting was multi layered. During the first hour of her first clearing session, I discovered that her Grandfather who resides in Heaven was a Shaman. I discovered she herself knew she was a gifted Psychic but had chosen not to work with her gifts. I also discovered she had been psychically attacked by a Spirit who had passed away but who did not cross over to Heaven. Some might call what was happening to her voodoo. People who were jealous of her were doing their best to keep her from God—people on 'this side and the other'. I went to work sending light in and around her until she herself felt better and more at peace. It was all I could do for her in that moment, as well as raise her awareness that she had disconnected from God. I cleared her aura, and cleared enough that she could hear herself. Her choice to disregard her powerful gift was keeping the malevolent entities within her. On the next few visits I was aware she had an internal possession. At times the voice of a woman would argue with me that was not her own. I performed a compassionate exorcism and asked Jesus to clear her on all levels in all dimensions and I prayed to release all jealous and disruptive malevolent entities and energies from her and her husband (who was also experiencing attacks). Each visit we discussed her gifts, and how she could work with them. Slowly but surely, she began working with herbs, and soon was sending me messages of how the herbs worked. The malevolent entities continued to disrupt her but no longer had any hold over her mind. She spontaneously released all remaining internal and external entities through her prayers, reconnection and awareness of God and began to experience the Divine on a constant basis. She moved out of a house that was haunted, burned a haunted CD, and reconnected to her powerful Gift.

Today, she is learning what it means to be a Medium with good boundaries. Her health is constantly improving, and has accepted her calling to clear and heal others.

In one case in 2016 I was asked to help with, a woman with bulimia and alcoholism who was possessed by 7 Spirits (externally as well as internally) who were demonizing her. During her clearing, I became aware that she was trying to vomit them out of her, and this had been the main reason she was inducing herself to vomit. She was attempting to purge herself.

While performing an exorcism on a woman who had been haunted most of her life, and demonized over 10 years, the demons inside of her spoke and told me they were from another planet. When I called their benevolent ancestors, who are in Heaven to take them home, they miraculously cleared out of the woman.

Probably the strangest encounter I've had was while a woman was under hypnosis for the purpose of weight loss. While under hypnosis a mean and nasty voice came out of the woman. She became very nasty and said things I won't repeat. She did not have any history of personality disorder or schizophrenia as far as I was aware. Because she did not come in for an exorcism I could not ethically perform an exorcism on her (although I REALLY wanted to). I believe she was possessed by her Mother from what I could gather. I prayed she would receive the healing she truly needed.

As a human being, I am limited by what I can do, however

God is not limited, God's Grace is UNLIMITED, God's

Mercy is Extraordinary,

And God's Love knows no Boundaries.

The Divine is our Birth Right

If you have not yet received God

Now is the time.

Forgiveness and Deliverance

Why is forgiveness so hard to do? It is one of the key
ingredients to a total healing. But why?

It is said that compassion is greater than love.
Through the heart, we find the avenue to the Soul–the deep
internal connection to Creator, and our capacity to feel God's
love. Through this love, we find the ability to love others,
and receive love from others. Compassion has an additional
element, it is formed through the capacity to feel deep
unconditional love. With the element of compassion one can
love another unconditionally, as Jesus did his apostle Paul.
With GREAT compassion God can heal us from our
unforgiveness. Unforgiveness can be healed. The power of
faith, prayer, and personal unraveling of deep hurts and pains
can bring about a spontaneous healing. It is a most
compassionate act to forgive oneself, and/or forgive another,
and it requires unconditional love or Divine Intervention.

94

With compassion one can feed the hungry, give money to the poor, reach greater depths of humanity, assist the sick, and offer deliverance. One develops compassion by deeply feeling and allowing God's love. By feeling God's unconditional love and experiencing the joy of God's love one can find the internal peace to love others unconditionally.

Through compassion one can finally be free of the pain of unforgiveness and when you are free of unforgiveness you are free to unlock the doors to all the joy that is waiting for you. Until you release it you are unable to see all it held from us. In essence, until it is released, it has power over your happiness.

Now you have heard me talk about the amazing power of forgiveness. Yet, it can be so hard to do. Forgiveness in my opinion is the magical tool in your toolbox to health, and often is the key to a full and total healing. Often forgiveness is held back because of fear–fear that once all is forgiven the problem will reoccur, or life will change Failure to forgive is often a shield used to prevent further pain. It is a breeding ground for self-doubt and shame. It can elicit the very thing you are trying to avoid–being overpowered, hurt, or possessed.

Yet why is it so hard to feel sometimes? When a person experiences deep hurts, pains, and disappointments it can be hard to feel unconditional love. One has to search to find it, yet it is always there. It is within our capacity to receive that we can open to the ever-present. Through the healing techniques in this book one can open up to receive, and once again feel God. Through receiving positive feelings and love from Creator, unconditional love can begin. Where there is unconditional love–there is forgiveness.

I personally had difficulty forgiving at one point in my past. I prayed to forgive and it did not come, so I sought the help of my elder and received a healing. I started to feel unconditional love once again and my capacity to forgive returning to me. Then I had a dream and an Ascended Master said 'you will come to know forgiveness'. Two weeks later I felt a complete release of emotions that I had been struggling with. Soon after I realized I was no longer harboring any feeling of unforgiveness.

In my personal experience I asked for help, remained in faith, and received a total clearing. This too is available for you.

Exorcism Prayer

Before starting this prayer, it is wise to follow a few simple instructions. No matter what your background these tools and prayers are Spiritual and Of The Light. With these prayers, powerful faith, words, Godly intentions, and a true clear heart to do God's work—a strong believer will invoke the Light of God and the Holy Spirit into a space, situation or person that is open and ready to receive it.

This prayer is for an internal as well as an external possession. Although the language implies it is for an internal possession, it will work well for an external possession, and usually an external possession will take considerably less time to clear. Sometimes an internal possession is not known, or is hidden, therefore it is advised to say a thorough prayer.

When you are ready to begin, it is wise to light a candle (white, black, or both if possible). Sage yourself and thoroughly sage the space to clear yourself and your energy. Call upon your Guides and God's Angels, Animal Totems, and Benevolent Heavenly Support.

Then, after lighting a candle, draw (invoke) a circle of God's Light (clockwise) around yourself three times using an imaginary piece of chalk in your hand or using actual salt **to include and protect yourself in the Light**, then draw (invoke) an imaginary circle of God's Light around your workspace or the room where you are three times using an imaginary piece of chalk in your hand or using actual salt **to include and protect all the people (and animals) in the room**. *Note, some may choose to use actual salt instead of imaginary chalk instead.*

At this point is very important to remove any unbelievers who are in the room (who are not the primary person receiving a clearing). If you do not remove the unbelievers from the room the clearing 'may' be blocked.

Mark the walls with Holy water if possible by making the sign of the cross in holy water on each of the four walls in each direction, and ask God to protect you.

Hang a branch of cedar (collected in a good way by giving back something to the earth, example hair or a penny) high up in the room for added assistance for a total healing.

Continue to leave sage burning in the room, and Osha root if it is available (or have it handy if possible) and burn sage as needed throughout the entire process.

Place a Bible in the room as well. Especially one with meaning to the practitioner, or an item of Spiritual significance.

Make sure you have your Ordained Ministers License or Certificate with you, and take the necessary time to answer any questions anyone might have to the best of your ability.

Wear clothes that cover head to toe, and protective jewelry, etc. Wear black clothing (so you can see the Light!) if possible. Wear a cross if one is available. Focus entirely on a positive experience, and make no promises. Focus on a time limit—depending on the situation one to two hours (however be prepared for listening to God's instructions). God is in charge.

Be of clear mind and clear heart, and humbly ask God to strengthen your faith 10,000 times more than you need it. This prayer is sacred, and is to be treated as such. Speak it out loud straight to GOD.

Ethical Wisdom

When performing any type of clearing work it is advised to follow the highest ethical code of conduct:

-Do as God asks you.

-Hold a Ministers License or Certificate (abide by the law).

-Be of Sound Mind. If you have been diagnosed with any type of mental health condition please consult with a spiritual person who does this work to determine your spiritual fitness. However, you can say these prayers for yourself, and should do so daily for protection.

-Follow the Ethics and Spiritual Teachings of Jesus.

-Harm No Living Person or Animal.

-Do No Harm to Yourself, your Spouse, or your Family.

-Live Clean and Sober.

-Connect to Spiritual Ego (God's will), not Personal Ego.

-Humbly Ask God for Guidance.

-Spend considerable amount of time in meditation and prayer on a regular basis.

-Prepare appropriately (at least 3 days before, as well as 3 days after is suggested) before any major clearing with: meditation, purification, strengthening, and rest (salt baths, rosary, prayer, sweat lodge, fasting, asking for forgiveness, forgive others, receive the Holy Spirit, remain vigilant, exorcise, and contemplate).

Increase your Faith.

Part One

A Call for The Light

I call forward Master Jesus, Benevolent Helpers, Legions of God's Angels, Archangel Michael, Archangel Gabriel, Archangels, Ascended Masters, and Benevolent Assistance from whatever realm available.

Part Two

Opening an Extraction Vortex

Great Spirit I humbly ask you to Open an Extraction Vortex now above _____ (name the location as well as the people's names who are present–see it above you on the ceiling) to Release all harmful things and malevolent energies, malevolent entities, and demons, malevolent archons, nests, malevolent portals, and harmful thought forms from the person(s) and place(s) named and us–and this Vortex shall remain as long as it is needed until all that is unclean is fully expelled and released from us and this place and person(s).

Thank you to the Elohim Angels and Seraphim Angels for your Spirals of Light cleaning up toxic energies in and around us now.

Part Three

Bringing A Soul to Light

"I Invite Your Soul _____ into the Circle"

If the person is present have them say their name aloud. If the person is not present and has verbally asked for this clearing, speak their name aloud. If the person is not present, and needs this type of healing say their name and wait until you receive confirmation from Spirit that they are in the circle and their will gives you permission (through vision, feeling, or an audible message from Great Spirit or your Guides/Angels). Proceed only with permission.

Say the Our Father Prayer **Three Times**

Use your intuition or a blessed pendulum to discern how many legal rights, demons, and entities need to be cleared.

If you are unsure - trust your instincts *and proceed with the entire process.*

See Page 205 Rules for Dowsing with a Pendulum

How many legal right are there to clear? ____

Is there a deliverance to occur? ____

How many demons are there to clear? ____

How many entities are there to clear? ____

Internal Possession? ____

External Possession? ____

Part Four

Cancelling All Unholy Legal Rights

Healer Speak Out Loud:

By Divine Force through the POWER of GOD,

God **clear now** the legal rights that have given any form of

darkness power over _____

(say the person's name aloud).

Restore _____ fully, in Jesus name!

I claim darkness, demons, and malevolent presences have

NO LEGAL RIGHTS to remain!

Have the person say out loud:

I claim darkness, demons, and malevolent presences have

NO LEGAL RIGHTS to remain! All rights I have ever given

harmful entities and energies are revoked!

I release you, release me NOW!

Have the person say out loud:

I _____ fully surrender to JESUS!

_____ has fully surrendered to JESUS!

(When you hear, or feel 'the permissions are revoked'

it is a sign all is clear and you can continue.)

Speak out loud to the person:

All malevolent energies are unbound from _____

and bound to Heaven.

All malevolent entities are unbound from _____

and bound to Heaven.

All Earthbound Non-Breathing Spirits that need to be

released in the highest health for all concerned are unbound

from _____ and released now to go with Jesus to Heaven.

All entities from all dimensions that need to be released in the

highest health for all concerned are

unbound from _____ and bound to Heaven.

All malevolent darkness is released from your physical

All malevolent darkness is released from your spiritual

All malevolent darkness is released from your emotional

All malevolent darkness is released from your mental self

All malevolent darkness is released from your aura

All malevolent darkness is released from your life

All malevolent darkness is released from your light

All malevolent darkness is released from your path

All malevolent darkness is released from your marriage
and your relationships

All malevolent darkness is released from your family

All malevolent darkness is released from your home

**Your Soul is claimed by God and you are claimed as a
Child of God, and you are hereby saved by God.**

Part Five

The Exorcism

ALTISSIMUM DEUS

DEUM EXCELSUM

The Most High God

DOMINUS DEUS SABBAOTH

Lord God of the Sabbath

PLENI SUNT COELI ET TERRA GLORIA TUA

Heaven and Earth are full of your Glory!

EGO SERVUS TUUS SUM ET HUMILIS

I am your humble servant

ET NUNC VENIO

Come now:

OMNIPOTENS DEUS

God Almighty

SPIRITUS SANCTUS

Holy Spirit

LESUS CHRISTI

Jesus Christ

FLAMMAM HYACINTHO

Violet Flame

OMNIUM SANCTORUM ET ANGELORUM DEORUM

All saints and God Angels

DE CAELO ET ARCHANGELIS

From Heaven and Archangels

EXERCITUS DOMINI ET NUNC VENI ET IN STATIONE CIRCA NOS

God's army station around us now

OB AUXILIUM EXIMITO

DAEMON/MALES SPIRITUM NUNC!

On account of take out the demon/malevolent spirit

ABSOLUTIO (RELEASE) AND

EXES, EXES, EXES (ERODE) THE UNCLEAN SPIRIT

NOW FROM YOUR CHILD _____

EXES EXES EXES THROUGH THE MOUTH NOW

BURN THE UNHOLY SPIRIT

WITH YOUR HOLY SPIRIT FIRE

DEUS, BURN THE UNCLEAN SPIRIT

IN YOUR FIERY FURNACE

DEUS, TRANSFER THE UNHOLY SPIRIT OUT OF

THE MOUTH OF _____

AND SEND IT THROUGH YOUR MERCY

STRAIGHT TO YOUR LIGHT IN HEAVEN,

YOUR FIERY FURNACE **IN HEAVEN-**THE VIOLET

FLAME OF GOD, OR THE PITS!

DEUS, TRANSFER THE UNCLEAN SPIRIT

AND IT NOT TRANSFER ANYWHERE ELSE!

UNLESS AS GOD COMMANDS IT

UNCLEAN SPIRIT, TRANSFER NOW AS GOD COMMANDS IT!

IESUS CHRISTI AMITTO MALE SPIRITUS / DAEMON

Jesus Christ send away malevolent spirits / demons

SPIRITUS BONI AB OMNIBUS PARTIBUS

Good Spirits assembled in all directions

DEORUM SANCTORUM IN LUMINE

By God's Holy Light

E TENEBRIS

Take out Darkness

ARCHANGELIS, DAEMONES!

Archangels, take the demons!

ET IN FLAMMAM HYACINTHO

Out into the Violet Flame

SPIRITUS SANCTUS IGNIS!

Holy Spirit Fire!

NULLI, NULLI REI

Harming No One (Living Person)

PENES ME PER VIRTUTEM DEI

By the power vested in me by God

ET EICIAM VOS DE DAEMONIBUS / SPIRITUS MALUS

I cast out of you demons/malevolent spirits

ABSOLUTIO!

Release!!!

DE ORE EIUS

Come out her/his mouth

QUO PRAECEPIT TIBI UT LESUM CHRISTUM

Go where Jesus Christ Commands you to Go!

EGO PRAECIPIO TIBI UT EXEAT!

I command you to come out (demons/malevolent spirits)!

OPORTET!

You (demons/malevolent spirits) must go!

NUMQUAM REDIRE

Never to return again

EJICITUR SPIRITUS MALUM VESTRUM

The Bad Spirit is cast out of you now

NIHIL PERMANERE

No Reason to Remain

Have the person being cleared speak out loud:

I release, through the power of God, I release all demons
and what is harming me, I revoke its power over me!
I claim my will is God's will—God has Power over my Soul!

To the person:

Through the Power of God, The Holy Spirit, and Jesus Christ all LEGAL RIGHTS any darkness, demons, and malevolent presences have are revoked now in this person and this place! Demons and malevolent presences have NO LEGAL RIGHTS here and cannot remain!

I draw out and bind YOU malevolent entities to Heaven's Violet Ray in the name of Jesus! Come out now harming no one and no thing! No Stone Unturned! You are cast out from this person, you are cast out of this person now!

DEUS AUTEM IMPLET LUX
The Light of God fills you!

RESTITUET PLENE IN LESUS CHRISTI!
Restore (this person) fully in Jesus Christ!

NIDOS OMNIA SUNT!
All nests are gone

OMNIA NOXIA IN PORTA CLAUSA EST!

All harmful portals are closed

TERRENUM QUIDEM OMNIA NON ENTIA SUNT

SPIRITUS SOLUTUS EX TE

All Earth Bound non breathing Spirits are released!

LIBERUM ARBITRIUM EST DE POSSESSIOE TUA

You/your will is free from possession

LUX AETERNA DEI PROSPERE AGIT ANIMA TUA

Your Soul is in The Light Of God

LIBERA NOS A MALO!

Deliver us from evil!

DEUS, GRATIAS AGO TIBI!

Thank you God!

DEUS, GRATIAS AGO TIBI!

Thank you God!

DEUS, GRATIAS AGO TIBI!

Thank you God!

ADDITIONAL CLEARING AS NEEDED

SPIRITUS SANCTUS REPLEVIT ME

The Holy Spirit fills me.

ET DIMITTE PECCATA

I remit the sins of this person

SPIRITUS SANCTUS IGNIS!

Holy Spirit Fire

BURN BURN BURN!

INCENDEMUS TE ET QUID SIT LIGARE!

Burn up what is binding you!

Through the Power VESTED In Me,

In THE NAME OF JESUS, through the POWER OF GOD

and the HOLY SPIRIT THAT FILLS ME

I cast out from you _____ and off of you all demons,

demonic entities, and attachments and cords, malevolent

spirits, betrayals, falsehoods, and negative energies! All these

things are hereby CAST out FROM you through your Mouth

NEVER TO RETURN AGAIN, cast OFF of you never to

return again, and cast from your life and those among you

never to return again! All these things cast out of you and

from you are cast into THE LIGHT, THE FIERY

FURNACE OF HEAVEN AND ARE NOT to

TRANSFER to anyone or anyplace else unless TO THE

PITS as Jesus Commands it!

Check the person to see how they are doing, if they need

water, if they need rest—lift up one of their arms and check to

see if it feels like they are 'back in their body'.

After a deliverance, a person will feel weak and clammy, and

sometimes will act like they have 'just returned', and 'don't' know what's going on' continue to assure them they are in God's hands, and that they are OK.

Give no power to any dark forms of conversation. Change the subject to God, Healing, and how good it feels to be clear. Focus all your intentions on a total deliverance harming no living person.
You are Connected, Your Faith is AMAZING.

Check their eyes–if their eyes are not clear (white), if their language is not clear, if you intuitively see 'black' in their mouth, if you can't 'see them' clearly, or if your instincts tell you to 'go on' then finish with this:

For the Healer to Speak

I am a believer.
In the name of Jesus Christ, the son of God, I exercise my authority and expel all evil spirits.
I command them to leave, according to the Word of God and in the name of Jesus. In the Name of Jesus, I bind the

malevolent principalities, harmful powers, rulers of darkness, spiritual wickedness, and all the strong demons into THE LIGHT and THE HOLY SPIRIT FIRE, or THE PITS.

I COMMAND all demons not to transfer, go exactly where Jesus wants you to go and do not come back.

I CANCEL ALL DEMONIC ASSIGNMENTS ON

_____.

In the name of Jesus I remit the sins of _____.

In the name of Jesus I command all unclean spirits to come out the mouth of _____.

In the name of Jesus I send Holy Spirit Fire in your body, over your body, and over the whole room—In the mighty name of Jesus Holy Spirit Fire Burns in you and over you from head to toe! The Light Fills You!

In the name of Jesus, I separate every unclean spirit from _____ soul in accordance to the Word of God.

I rebuke and cast out every unclean spirit to the pit or the FIRES of HEAVEN and THE LIGHT wherever they

SHOULD GO per GOD, and command them never return again in Jesus name.

Warrior Angels, hook into the demons and take them to the PIT, or to the FIRES of HEAVEN and THE LIGHT wherever they should go as Jesus commands.

I cut all evil spiritual connections to this body and burn it away in the name of Jesus.

Burn NOW!

I loose burning judgment and destruction upon you unclean spirits in the name of Jesus.

Part Six

Cutting of Cords

ARCHANGEL MICHAEL

with your SHIELD and SWORD

Cut away the cords and attachments from _____ to

unholy spirits now, unholy entities, and unholy energies now!

Release what is harming _____ now!

Release what needs to be released now!

Shield us from all evil and demonic attacks.

MICHAEL ARCHANGELE APERITE PORTAS

Archangel Michael Open the Gates

(to Heaven to release what/who else needs to be released)

Thank you God for your Swift Deliverance

Thank you Archangel Michael for

your mighty Shield and Sword.

MOTHER TERESA

I humbly beckon you to cut the cords to sickness and disease,
and release the sickness and disease that ever gave this
darkness a place to rest–cure the disharmony and disease
and bring peace and light to fill this person now.

Great Spirit God Almighty Deliver us from evil
and Restore us in God's Grace! Clear us and restore us with
waves of Healing Light!

Allow the flow of positive healing energy from God's Light
to pour into yourself and the person being healed.

Say out loud

I call waves of Healing Light
Thank you for this healing.

Part Seven

Spiritual Healing

OMNIA DIMITTENTUR A DEO

All is forgiven by God

IACET OMNIBUS REVOCANDA SUNT!

All lies are revoked!

SANITAS! NUNC SANITAS!

Sanity Now!

Have the person receiving the healing repeat after you:

I believe in Great Spirit, the Father of Heaven and Earth.

I believe in Jesus, the Benevolent Christ Ray, Angels, and The
Holy Realms of Heaven.

I confess all my sins and repent.

I forgive everyone who has hurt me from this life,
or any past life.

I ask for forgiveness for anytime I was misunderstood, or I
misunderstood and became sick.

I ask for forgiveness for anytime my EGO stood between me
and You God. I release all unforgiveness and ill will now
with God's help, by the grace of God.

I claim my EGO is now a Spiritual Godly EGO that never
interferes with your work in me.

I transfer all my pain, fear, rejection, abandonment, betrayal,
mistrust, and abuse to the cross of Jesus Christ.

Father GOD please forgive me, and bring me to peace. I
receive peace now.

I renounce pride, and know it is an abomination to You.

I renounce rebellion, stubbornness, disobedience, self-hatred,
and self-centeredness.

I humbly call my way back to you now God.
I humble myself and come to You as a child and ask for
forgiveness and deliverance, in the name of Jesus.

I renounce unbelief, doubt, fear, lies, hatred, unfaithfulness,
and anger.

All betrayals are forgiven—from all lines on my mother's side
all the way back to Adam and Eve (or before if needed.) as
well as my Father's side all the way back to Adam and Eve (or
before if needed).

I renounce, break, and loose myself from ALL demonic subjection to my parents or any human being living or dead, or alien, or other dimensional being who has dominated me in any way against the will of God.

Thank you, God, for setting me free.

I AM FREE

I AM FREE

I AM FREE

In Jesus I am Free

Part Eight

Restoring God's Blessings

All malevolent sources are ordered
to loose now:

all natural resources, land, home(s), animals, money, career,
our name (s), life force energy, reputation, health
(and for those souls in my life that agree to this), marriage
and family bonds, relationships, the health of those in our
family, as well as the finances of people who owe us money,
and all the things you have stolen from my family that are
ours through the blessings of Jesus.

Father, please send Your angels to bring all these things back
to us in whatever way you choose is best, harming no one
and no thing. God, protect restore and protect our blessings
that have been given to us by you.

Part Nine

Rejoicing In The Light

May you _____ be blessed and know you are cherished!

May you humbly cherish your life now
and all your days ahead in all its goodness as the Light of God
is IN YOU NOW and FOREVER. May the Glory of GOD
be with you always. May you always and forever
be protected by God.

I am always and forever protected by God!
You are always and forever protected by God!
I call forward the Rainbow Light, God's Light,
Love Light, Happy Light, Healing Light,
Awakened Universal Consciousness Light, Oneness Light,
Archangel Gabriel's Healing Green Light, Archangel
Michaels's Protective Blue Light – restore us on all levels and
return to us through God's grace what is needed now!

Restore us to Sanity!
By God's Holy Light I am a Child of Light
Never to return to fear and ego again.

A walk of Faith and Trust shall light my path
And follow me wherever I shall go.

To the Hollow Bone

(The Healer who spoke this Prayer)

A shield of glory

A thousand angels sing your praise

May the Glory of God follow you all your days!

Victory, Victory, Victory!

God's Light Shines in you, on you,

all your Days.

Clearing Prayers

Who can channel healing? Anyone!

Hands-on healing is one of the oldest forms of clearing, and the power of touch to heal is ages old and found in every culture. One form of healing is called Reiki. In 1922 Doctor Mikao Usui, a Japanese Buddhist, revived the ancient healing practice of Reiki–a form of healing that goes back to the time of Jesus Christ, and possibly was used during the time of Jesus. Reiki arrived in the United States in 1937 and in the 70's Reiki Master Hawayo Takata began training students in Reiki all the way to Reiki Master. Since that time, the sacred ancient practice of Reiki has found its way into hospitals, wellness centers, private practice, church's, and is offered remotely by healers as well. Anyone who is attuned to the Holy Spirit can offer healing through the hands. Reiki assists the healer to be a clear channel, and through Reiki a healer can more easily harness, and direct the energy. In addition, the Reiki Practitioner benefits greatly with this method as the Practitioner is able to release toxic energy from himself/herself and others and remain clear. Without this knowing, some healers become ill from taking on others sickness. God does not intend for us to become sick when we help others. In old times, Healers took on the sickness of others, then became sick themselves and often died early. Today, that is no longer necessary. We have the tools to remain clear. When a practitioner is taking on too much energy of others it is a clear sign they are in need of some rest.

As God's Light comes through a minister, healer, etc. God is able to heal a person, place, of situation.

Prayers and Intentions are one and the same. Through powerful words spoken with a true heart–God is able to heal, clear, and work miracles through the words and intentions of one who is called to do the work of God.

Following is a small compilation of clearing prayers and hands on healing techniques that can be spoken for the benefit of healing a person, a home, a situation. Healing is only limited to where you limit it. God is everywhere, and in everything.

When and How to Clear A House

There are many ways to clear a house, as there are many prayers for exorcism, clearing, and healing. The way that works most effectively is still the best way – the old way. I suggest that anyone who is going to clear a house or a person, must first be an Ordained Minister, and follow the laws governing the Ministers in their respective state of dwelling. Second, do not skimp on the tried and true basics that work. Good prayers equal good results.

There are many aspects to clearing a home. No two homes are alike. The walls of the home are like the bones of a body, and the bones have a memory. The bones of a home contain memories of every person who has ever lived there, every family, every joyous occasion, every birth, every wedding, every haunting, every argument, every trauma, and every death.

When a person is experiencing sickness, disease, fatigue, memory loss, headaches/migraines, depression, addiction, insomnia, and general unhappiness or unease–it is my recommendation to clear the house. When a person is experiencing a possession (internal or external), the home should be cleared if possible before the person is cleared. When animals are experiencing anxiety, excessive peeing, excessive barking, staring at blank walls, or acting strangely– it is probably a good idea to clear the house.

When children are having nightmares, experience seeing ghostly Spirits, are nervous, bedwetting, afraid to sleep in their own bed–it is also a good idea to clear the house, and include them in the clearing. Including children in a house clearing shows them that their parents care about their well-being and gives them a sense of empowerment over their situation. It has been my experience when a child experiences a haunting and you include them in the house clearing they experience a feeling of safety as they watch their parents and helpers clear the house, and are often quick to step in and participate in the clearing (shaking a rattle, sprinkling salt, singing a happy song). When the entire family becomes empowered together it is a Spiritual Healing, and keeping the home clear becomes second nature when the family is working together.

First, all members of household must be present (whenever possible, and if it is not possible–gain their consent for the Shaman, Minister, or Priest to clear the house.)

1) All members of the family gather in the central gathering place of the home and hold hands in a circle and say a prayer to open the circle for the house to be clear and call forward Great Spirit, the Benevolent Angels, Ancestors, Totems, Guides, and Spirits who can clear the house now of all non-breathing earth bound Spirits and malevolent entities and energies to come forward to clear the house on your behalf. The family members should say what they are grateful for, and have an attitude of team-work.

2) Ask the Elohim and Seraphim Angels to open an Extraction Vortex above the home to release what needs

to be released during the clearing for the highest health of all, according to God.

3) Have the Mother/Father or main leaseholders or owner stand on the front porch–light some sage in a fireproof container (iron pot, shell, small cauldron). Make sure if anyone who has breathing problems or is pregnant, nursing, or has any aversion to sage that they stay outside and away from the sage during the clearing–they can stay outside and pray during the clearing until the smoke has cleared. Sage all members of the family and then the front door and ask that from here forward only good benevolent Spirits can pass through the doorway, ask the Ancestors to bless the doorway (sprinkle salt, lavender, and/or holy water on the threshold as well if desired), and state out loud that you are the owner/leaseholder and anyone who is not on the lease or who is not a family member, or who is not allowed in the house (all non-breathing earth bound Spirits) must leave now by the Power of Great Spirit. It is good to wear a cross and

have a cross in the home (or other equally Spiritual item) during the clearing.

4) Begin saging the home–go through every room ceiling to floor, corner to corner, and let the medicine of the smoke clear the home. Go in every closet, big room, stairwell, and small room. Where there are 'cold spots' pray out loud for Archangel Michael to 'clear this house'!

5) When finished end at the back door of the home–sage the doorway and say prayers for protection–then with the door open command all unwelcome Spirits and non-breathing Earth Bound Spirits and negative energies and entities to leave 'out the back door and go where Jesus commands you to go harming no one and no thing (and wait a few minutes as the energy goes out the door). With a strong tone in your voice direct all that does not belong there to leave. Sage the back door again.

6) Say a closing prayer of Gratitude and Thanks to Great Spirit (GOD), and say 'to those who need to go GO, and

Thank You!, to those benevolent helpers who need to stay who can ensure this home is clear, STAY Thank You! It is **very important** to complete the process by releasing the benevolent helper Spirits who helped you. Thank you, Archangel Michael, and the Elohim and Seraphim Angels! Ask that all portals and vortexes that need to be closed now in the highest health close now. Have everyone speak their intentions for how they want the home to feel now that it is clear (happy, more positive energy, etc.). Then everyone go about their day as usual.

Tips:

Place small cups of salt around the home in places where it is safe to the people and pets who live there. Placing one cup in each corner of the home (on the floor, or counter/shelf whichever is best and most convenient—as many as you are 'called' to place around the home) prior to a house clearing assists with the clearing. Before or during the clearing salt the window sills and doorways. Replace as needed.

Keep incense and candles burning for a few days as needed prior to the clearing to help raise the vibration.

Have sacred items handy (a Bible, Holy water, lavender, a cross, crystal, Nordic shield, rattle, drum, feather fan, etc.) for the clearing – items that are unique to your family, a picture of a beloved Grandmother/Grandfather.

Pets love house clearing, they are the best helpers.

When children are present, you can offer to give them a clear quartz crystal to place in their bedroom to remind them of the clearing.

Before and after the clearing play music the family loves.

Keep all EMF (electronics) to a minimum for a while if possible.

Keep all weapons stored away, not hanging on walls if at all possible–create a more peaceful environment.

Hang Swarovski crystals in windows to bring in more Light.

Wash curtains and draperies, as well as bed spreads and bedding more often for a while.

Place a beautiful amethyst crystal in the central gathering place of the home–and ask it to be your family's protector.

Spray straight vinegar in a spot where activity is most felt, and see if that helps–it should. If it does help spray it wherever else you need to (keeping in mind not to stain anything of value with the vinegar and be careful of pets and people). After spraying vinegar–burn some sage or incense in the same spot. Repeat as needed.

Wash mirrors with lemon water that has a touch of vinegar and salt in it to close 'mirror portals'.

Use Holy water to make the sign of the cross (or other Spiritual Symbol unique to you) on every door, window, and mirror in the house.

Burn Sweet Grass once a day for several days after the clearing (or when you think about it) to invite the Good Spirits and keep positive vibes high in the house.

Keep a fountain in the home, and add some Holy water to it to 'keep the Holy Spirit flowing in your home'.

Spray/spritz the home with a container that has been saged and blessed and filled with homemade clearing mist made of blessed water, a few sage leaves, a small dash of salt, a drop of vinegar, and a few drops of aromatherapy (frankincense, lemon, lavender, pine, dragons blood scent, garlic oil, or any kind of aromatherapy used for clearing and purification that you prefer and is safe to all family members and pets).

You can find most of these ingredients at your local metaphysical retail store, herbal tea store, or whole food/health food market.

Prayer to Keep a Home Clear

No unclean Spirit may enter this house (office, apartment, etc.) or this person _____ (say their name aloud). This now and forever more is a place of God. This now and forever more is a person of God. God claims this house, God is in this house, God protects this house and the land beneath, and the sky above–and all those who dwell in it shall have peace and all those who come when here shall have peace. God claims the person (s) named, and their energy, the land beneath, and the sky above them.

All harmful energies he/she/they comes in contact with will not be able to transfer onto, or into this person, or this person's aura, energy, or belongings.

Harmful energy no longer exists in this place. Harmful energy no longer exists in or on this person, or this person's aura. This home is clear, and stays clear now in Jesus name.

The portal of Divine Source energy flows positive energy, joy, health, and abundance freely in this house now.

We claim Jesus in all corners of this house now.

Through the Power of God, Jesus Christ and the Holy Spirit- All portals where malevolent energy has come – malevolent energy and entities are returned now back through the portal from which it came – the portal is sealed and you are never to return again. Dear God, I humbly request that you station your Angels at the doors and windows of this dwelling–on the inside as well as the outside and watch over and protect us all our days.

Prayer to Keep a Person Clear

No unclean Spirit may enter this person _____ (say their name aloud). This now and forever more is a person of God. God claims this person, this person's energy, this person's home, car, and office/work space, title, the land beneath, and the sky above this person – and all harmful energies this person comes in contact with will not be able to transfer onto, or into this person, or this person's aura or energy, or belongings. Harmful energy no longer exists in or on this person, or in this person's aura.

This person is clear, and stays clear now in Jesus name. This person claims Divine Source energy as (his/her) inherent right, and love and positive flows of energy, health, and abundance flow freely for this person now.

Have the person say out loud:

I claim God as the One True Divine Source

God is the Light and the Truth!

God help me, heal me, and protect me now and always

Remove the nests from me now,

Heal my aura now,

Wherever leaks exist for harmful energy–I ask the leaks are

sealed now in and around my life.

Heal me from lies and manipulations now.

God, I humbly request that you station your Angels around

me now and protect me always

In Your Light.

Binding the Ahab, Jezebel, Succubus, and Incubus

This is a powerful prayer and not to be taken lightly. If you begin to pray it and a person has an adverse or negative reaction to one, two, or all three of these words take note on which word they are having the reaction to. If they react to Ahab, someone in their life or they are possessed with Ahab psychic attack—a man who is not taking responsibility for their family and not acting as the spiritual leader of their family. If they react to Jezebel (Ahab's Wife) they are or a female they know is possessed with unethical and immoral behavior. If they react to Succubus, someone in their life, or they are being psychically attacked by a female succubus (dark spirit possessing a woman to seduce a man and break up a spiritual union intended to prevent a spiritual person from his or her power—usually one who would have great Spiritual impact on a community—usually a woman of great standing) or an Incubus (dark spirit possessing a man or demonizing a man to seducing a woman (or women) intended to prevent this man from his Spiritual self, break up a Spiritual union, or steal his power so he cannot positively Spiritually influence his community). I recommend study of the Biblical understanding of these words. If someone in a family line has been possessed with this type of energy, it may be handed down—and may be a family curse. Give no power to it, say the prayers, and live a good life.

Binding the Ahab, Jezebel, Succubus, and Incubus Prayer

Jesus and Archangel Michael, Bind and remove the Ahab, the Jezebel, the Succubus and Incubus from _____ (the person's name) now. God removes these unholy abominations now from you & your family line all the way back to Adam and Eve. All the malevolent Ahab, Jezebel, Succubus, and Incubus cords are cut from you.

Ahab Leave this person now. The Ahab is bound away from you now and bound into the Violet Ray.

Jezebel leave this person now. The Jezebel is bound away from you now and bound into the Violet Ray.

Succubus and Incubus leave this person now. The Succubus and Incubus are bound away from you now and bound into the Violet Ray.

The Ahab, the Jezebel, and the Succubus and Incubus
are bound away from you into the Violet Ray
through the Power of God.
All Ahab, Jezebel, Succubus, and Incubus energies and
entities are hereby removed and cast out of you, cut from you
and your life-with God's Holy Knife as well as your family
line all the way back to Adam and Eve.

In Jesus name, Ahab, Jezebel, Succubus, and Incubus
have no legal rights to remain.

Removing Malevolent Ruler Spirits
Of a Person

Through the Power vested in me through Creator and in the
name of Jesus, ALL malevolent ruler spirits of
_____ (speak the person's name/family
name) ARE HEREBY REMOVED,
and FOREVER BOUND to HEAVEN!!!

This person and their life, marriage(s), children, home, jobs,
vehicles, friends, businesses/careers, family & extended
family, town, city ARE CLEARED – are FULLY clearing
NOW–RESTORED through the blood of CHRIST!

Light fills you now all your days!

Removing Malevolent Ruler Spirits
Of a Place

Through the Power vested in me through Creator and in the
name of Jesus, ALL malevolent ruler spirits of
_____ (speak the place/community name)
ARE HEREBY REMOVED from this place,
and FOREVER BOUND to HEAVEN!!!

This place and all the people who
live/work/inhabit/visit/come to this place ARE CLEARED,
and hereby RESTORED through the blood of CHRIST!

God's Love and Light flows powerfully into this place,
and fills this place now and always.

Claiming God In Your Life

God is in me, God is in my spouse/partner, God is in our family, God is in our Health, God is in our wallets, God is in our House (Apartment, Townhouse, Condo, etc.), God is in our Children, God is in our Lives, God is in our marriage, God is in our Jobs, God is in our relationships, God is in the day, and God's light fills the night, God is in our Businesses/Career/ Jobs, God is in our pets, God is in our property.

GOD's LIGHT SHINES IN AND ON US NOW

Negative Block of Issue

_____ (state the

issue out loud)

I AM. I AM LOVE. I AM FREE OF
NEGATIVITY/BLOCKS STATED/LISTED ABOVE!

The Lighted 13

You and the Holy Trinity are the Foundation of Earth

The Connection of God on Earth

The Truth is Light

The Cornerstones of Goodness:

Clarity, Integrity, Honesty, Wisdom

God has claimed the Earth

Malevolent beings can no longer exist here

God has claimed the ONE and the THREE

The Ten and the Thirty, and The Thirty ONE

And the Thirteen are claimed by God

Restored to God's Grace

And cannot be used by malevolent sources.

All numbers are claimed by God and restored in God's
Grace,

Used in THE LIGHT and hereby and forever FROM THE
LIGHT only.

Colors

I claim all colors

are restored in God's Grace,

Used in THE LIGHT and hereby and forever FROM THE
LIGHT only.

Spirit Fire

Holy Spirit Fire

Burns in and around us night and day

Burning harmful darkness into the Violet Ray!

Into The Violet Light

The harmful darkness goes out like a tide

Into the Violet Light - Never to return again!

Thank you Archangel Michael!!!

Thank you Archangel Gabriel!!!

Thank you Saint Germaine!!!

Healing Prayers

This next Prayer, **The Emotional Release Prayer,** I have used successfully for many years. It is an ancient Buddhist practice of releasing negative energy to 'open the channels to release' I have added the Prayers as I heard them from Great Spirit. Combined together, the releasement and the Prayer–this technique becomes a powerful releasement tool and should only be done when someone wants it and agrees to it verbally. This is a wonderful self-healing tool as well.

Once you open your channels to release you can then learn to receive at a higher vibration.

I have joked for years and said our Bodies are like a toilet with Energy flowing into it all the time. That is why I reverently, and lovingly call this next Prayer "Flushing the Toilet"

This EMOTIONAL RELEASE Prayer is a powerful stand-alone tool used to cleanse and release toxic emotions. For those sick only with emotional pain this may be all they need. For those infected with entities, continue on to the additional prayer—or if it is obvious, skip right to the Exorcism Prayer. If you are unsure, this is a good place to start.

Emotional Release Prayer

To release excess energy, Other People's Energy, and Clear the Path for Fresh New Energy to come in.

How much a person releases is up them and God.

Have the person sit straight up in a chair
To receive the healing.

Keep your distance from the person, a hand on the shoulder is fine as long as they consent and you are an Ordained Minister. Give them space to do their work.

Ask them to breathe as if breathing up into their shoulders and 'down their arms' letting the energy OUT the palms of the hands.

Their mind may not understand this however trust that the body will. **Hands should be facing the earth, comfortably as possible. Have them Breathe Deeply 'up into the shoulders and out the hands' three times or until you feel that energy is releasing and the person's release channel is OPEN.**

Now have them breathe easily and lightly keeping the channels open to release. Breathing lightly and easily up into the shoulders, from the shoulders down through the arms, releasing energy down through the palms of the hands, letting it all go—releasing it to the earth mother who can lovingly receive it.

Tell them to 'Stay Open'
And 'Breathe Easily Now'

You will begin to see and possibly feel the flow of energy up and out, and it is usually very relaxing to the person receiving healing, their posture may relax some—remind them to stay sitting straight up if necessary. For those healers who work with the Chakra system, you are opening up the Kundalini (flow of divine awakening energy within) at the heart.

Speak this out loud to the person:

God, please clear the pain from this person now that can be released harming no one and no thing.

God, please clear the grief from this person now that can be released harming no one and no thing.

God, please clear the guilt from this person now that can be released harming no one and no thing.

God, please clear the anger from this person now that can be released harming no one and no thing.
(Anger is a big one and may take server minutes to clear)

God, please clear the judgment of self from this person now that can be released harming no one and no thing.

God, please clear the judgment of others from this person now that can be released harming no one and no thing.

God, please clear the self-loathing and depression from this person now that can be released harming no one and no thing.

God, please clear the shame from this person now that can be released harming no one and no thing.

God, please clear the fear from this person now that can be released harming no one and no thing.

God, please clear the stress from this person now that can be released harming no one and no thing.

God, please clear the anxiety from this person now that can be released harming no one and no thing.

God, please clear the worry from this person now that can be released harming no one and no thing.

Let them finish releasing.

When they are done releasing:
Stand behind the person
And now place one of your hands on the back of their neck and imagine healing light coming down into their neck and in through the crown of their head and say:

LIGHT FILLS YOU NOW
PEACE FILLS YOU NOW

Stand for a few minutes receiving positive energy and God's Pure Light and sending energy to the person.

Have them brush off (I tell people to shake their arms or I use a feather fan to brush them off) their arms, their chest, and, if needed, the top of their head.

At this point it is a good idea to sage if safe to do so.

If sageing is indicated (check to make sure not nursing, pregnant, etc. otherwise sageing is contraindicated for health reasons).

Have them receive grounding energy by imagining pulling Earth energy up through the feet from the Earth, and breathe easily.

Karmic Clearing Prayer

Place one hand on the chest either over the heart of where you feel 'emotional' (or place the hands and wrists facing downward on or above the knee) and breathe lightly with a "puh puh" breath. Relax and go into a light meditative state. Now imagine a movie screen is playing on your forehead (your third eye just above the middle of the eye brows). While breathing lightly "puh puh puh puh puh... etc." allow memories to surface on the movie screen and watch them without judgment. As you watch them become aware they are releasing with every "puh" breathe. The memory will release and more will surface as long as you are still and allowing the movie screen will play.

Breathe, release the memory, move on to the next.
Stay 'in the memory that is difficult' as long as needed.

You may see happy memories and sad memories–you may see today's memories or yesterdays–or anytime in this life or another life. If a memory stays a long time allow it to stay until it releases and continue to breathe through it. Allow at least 20 minutes when starting out, twice a day for two weeks is recommended. Graduate to 10 minutes per day after two weeks, and as needed. Many things that need to be released will surface—some may be surprising.

"I Release" Prayer

Place one or both hands over your heart and say "I Release" out loud—state the first emotion that comes to you. Then "I Release the emotion _____". With your hand over your heart allow the memory attached to the emotion to surface. Keep your hand over your chest (where surface emotions are stored). As you see or hear or feel the memory—the harmful attachments to this memory are released. Memories that surface may be this life or past life. Stay in non-judgment and self-love. Wisdom that comes through brings healing situations in your life now that are tied to the emotions of the past. A person may also naturally develop a greater understanding of how past lives affect us in the present.

Heal Me at the ROOT, Jesus

Dear God, ruler of Heaven and Earth, please heal my scars of
unfaithfulness and dis-ease.

Seed thoughts and feelings that benefit my new life now in
me. Heal all of me, Heavenly Father.

Through your mercy all scars are revealed and healed. At the
core, I ask JESUS to dig up all roots of dis-ease. I allow all
roots of the pain/situation to be hereby CAST OUT and
removed. I am filled and seeded anew with FAITH in GOD,
Faith in God's LOVE for me, and Faith in myself.

God's Light fills me. I accept pleasant and helpful, beneficial
energies and JOY now grows within me, my life, my heart,
my mind–and paves my path–lit by the Divine.

My True Nature

(Use Citrine to strengthen your core connection with God and repeat this with your hand on your core/stomach). This prayer is used for depression, feelings of hopelessness and suicidal thoughts, and despair —as well as healing broken connections and strengthening connections from your core to The Creator.

Say it over and over as needed.

My true nature is a brightly burning flame!
Ever connected to the God of
ALL GOOD THINGS.

I am a Butterfly

My soul expands in the Light

I dance free–I harness no emotion that would keep me from

thee–Divine

I breathe, and I breathe, and I breathe

I expand, and I am free

Positive

Positive Energy

Raising The Vibration

God's Light

I am In Participation!

Taking my Power Back

Great Spirit

Recover my power from any time, any place, and any person where I ever lost my power. Recover and restore my power from anyone I ever gave my power away to. Help me to forgive myself. I forgive myself now with God's help. I forgive anyone who took my power. God entrust me now with the power YOU want me to have–give me the strength to claim it, receive it as my own, and make benevolent use of it always. Protect me now and always and help me to have the right authority as directed by God. All power I ever lost is restored.

I trust myself with this power as it is entrusted in me.

I am a powerful bright being of God's Light.

Prayers for Addicts

In my lifetime, I have known addiction and known addicts. Through God's love and mercy, I have healed from addiction and I have witnessed many heal from addiction. Yet, many still suffer. With every form of suffering there is a purpose.

I have seen many ways to heal from addiction—but none of them included a lack of spirituality. All forms of healing from addiction include God. And God is the missing ingredient where there is addiction. All forms of addiction are an attack of the will. All forms of healing from addiction are a recovery of the Godly will—your true purpose.

Through the years, I have worked with many who are afflicted and have worked through readings, healings, shamanic healing, and hypnosis to heal the will—as God has shown me, and in each case it is different. The root cause of the sick will is different in every case. In in every case the healing is unique. For some it may take years of therapy searching for the answers. Ultimately the answer comes only when the person afflicted is ready to receive God and their divine purpose. When a person recovers their true nature and their Godly will—the change is instant.

Through their addiction and through their suffering and the recovery of their Godly Will, many Spiritual people have risen through the ashes to become powerful leaders, healers, and ministers. Through their suffering and through their death's—many beautiful Souls have become great helpers and healers in the Spirit world. We cannot fully understand God's plan.

If you or someone you know is experiencing addiction. These prayers came to me to be added to this book. If someone comes in for clearing due to their nature of being addicted (it is usual for addicted people to pick up earthbound Spirits and possibly demons during their travels) once the clearing occurs they will continue to pick up harmful toxic energy until they are free of the addiction. I urge anyone suffering with addiction to say this simple prayer 'Jesus, take away 100% of my cravings, and heal anything that has caused it, restore me to sanity, restore my will, and restore my health'. Get into a program (AA, NA, Church, Talk Therapy Group, Etc.) with others, even if your cravings have subsided or are gone, and know your experience has purpose —and you are here to help others heal from an afflicted will.

Recover Now

Dear God, Please recover _____ Bring him/her to a place of recovery within himself/herself. Please help him/her recover the pieces of himself/herself that he/she has lost. Help him/her to regain control over himself/herself, his/her body, his/her will, his/her mind, his/her emotions, and become conscious of what he/she needs now for healing and health – and able to receive it. Help him/her to align to you, OH GOD through whose love all things are made possible.

Please help him/her receive the REALIZATION *they need* (harming no one and no thing if possible) to receive in order for his/her recovery to begin now.

Faith for You

Even though you have lost control,

I'm in control of myself,

and I Have Faith you will gain control.

Even though you are addicted to _____

And consuming things that are harmful to you,

I'm free of cravings for _____

And consuming things that are healthy to me.

I Have Faith you will be free of cravings

And will consume things that are healthy for you.

Even though you have mental, emotional, physical,

and / or spiritual problems

I am healthy on all levels.

I Have Faith you're getting healthy on all levels.

Darkness I Invite You in To The Light

Darkness that exists wherever you are in my life–may love find you now unconditionally. Jesus please send Angels of LOVE now to embrace the places deep within my soul that have attracted this addiction–bring it INTO THE LIGHT. Jesus please send Angels of MERCY now to embrace the places deep within me that cannot give up–and help me to surrender fully and completely this addiction and all cravings associated with it–to you now Jesus.

I repent my sins, I release my shame, I let go of my ego that says I can do it alone, I gather myself with dignity,

And I start fresh–now–in YOU God.

Today,

I AM CLEAN.

Heal My Harmful Patterns

God heal me from any time I've abandoned myself, or
anytime I abandoned others undeserving of my
abandonment, because I abandoned you God and myself, and
what was good for my soul and my life.
Forgive me for when I could not receive goodness.
I ask for healing and deep forgiveness.
I ask God to miraculously heal my abandonment Karma, and
heal the deep wounds in anyone I have injured.
God heal now the abandonment, rejection, and denial
patterns within me. I am in FAITH that you are with me,
and I shall never be alone. Heal me from anytime I rejected
you God and anytime I rejected myself and what is good for
me and my soul. Forgive me of all my sins and restore me in
my heart to receive the divine love that you, oh Creator
intended for me–and help me to receive this love and this life
you have bestowed on me in full.

Living in The Truth

Creator I live now in the Truth.

Forgive me for any time I didn't want to know you.

Forgive me for not wanting to see you and acknowledge how you're working in my life. Heal me from my deprivation of you. Forgive me for denying the truth. Release me from subjugation to lies I was told or that I told myself that held me from you. Release information I heard that was incorrect about You. Thank You, I'm Sorry, I love You.

The truth is You, the truth is in Me.

Prayers for Mediums

Blessed be the ones who are 'OF THE SOUL'!
The word Psychic means literally 'of the soul' – the animal
totem for the soul is the butterfly. Those who are of the soul
are the transformers–and through our own personal
transformations and growth many are healed. A person can
become open to the Spirit world in many ways. The ways a
person can become a psychic medium is through growing up
in a home with an addict, through abuse, through ptsd, by
working in the military or experiencing war. There are also
the more traditional ways–meditation, a past life as a spiritual
person, praying for an awakening, working as a yoga
practitioner, etc, and through working as a healer (nurse,
doctor, chiropractor, massage therapist, etc.). Becoming
aware of your Soul, your Soul's purpose, and the Divine as
the Divine works through you is a powerful awakening.
These prayers are intended to keep you safe.

Clear Me Now Jesus!

God protect me from being possessed

by anyone or anything.

Clear me now Jesus.

Strengthen my armor and keep me clear.

God in you, and through you

I am a sovereign being.

I exist now and always

of and From the Light.

My Light body is clear of toxic energy.

Archangel Michael's sword and shield are activated within my

armor.

Through Jesus and the Power of God and The Holy Spirit I

am free and clear of all external and internal possessive

energies/entities/thought forms/demons/and anything

that would be harmful to my being or is harming me now

or was ever harming me, possessing me, or was trying to possess me. All is peaceful and in harmony with God in my mind, my heart, my body, my Spirit, and my Soul.

Prayer for Control over
Your Physical Body

God, please forgive me for any time I let someone come into
my physical body (my aura, my life, my energy) that is not in
my highest health. Thank you for preventing harm from
coming to me. Thank you for your protection God on all
levels and in all dimensions. Show me what I can do to be
even more protected – I know I am special in your eyes.
Raise my awareness and my discernment for my highest
good.
Surround me in your loving safety net now and always.
God, please forgive me for any time I let someone or
something have control over me, my mind, my spirit.

Thank you for clearing me and preventing it from happening
ever again. Thank you for releasing negative emotions
influencing my behavior.

God please forgive me for anytime I allowed a person to hurt me or harm me—or anytime I harmed myself or felt I had no control over myself (or from harming myself).

For anytime I was victimized, abused, traumatized, raped, kidnapped, abducted, or harmed in anyway by another person —in this life or any past life—God heal all parts of my soul and free me from my captors. Deliver ME NOW in God's Light through your Mercy.

Increase my interest in the Divine. Divine Power flows to me and through me for the benefit of myself and others. I am now aligned in God and with God.

My Faith in God is restored.

I deeply and completely trust myself.

My belief in the good of mankind is restored.

I have a healthy life now and always – and for the rest of my days. I am in control of my be-ing through the Power of God who has all control.

My be-ing is at Peace.

I am playful.

I am intuitive.

I am at ease.

Gentle Reminder Prayer

I do not clear people, God Clears People.

I do not heal people, God Heals People.

God clears and heals people.

If a Person Does not clear,

I do not take it personally.

I remove my ego.

My Intentions are Powerful.

My Prayers are Good.

I do as God directs me to Do.

I do not harm myself or others.

I am benevolent – a soldier of God.

I have no control over God's Divine Plan,

Nor do I have control over God's Divine Interventions.

My voice is strong, my words are powerful.

My Prayers are heard.

I trust in God's Infinite Wisdom.

I take every day one day at a time, and feel God's Love.

I take care of myself, and tend to my own issues.

My house is in order.

3 Step Rebirthing & Balancing Prayer

Step One

"I am _____ (state your full name)

Nothing, other than God, can co-exist in my body.

Only MY Spirit resides in my body."

Step Two

Take several deep controlled slow breaths.

"I call God into my body, heart, mind, and soul."

Balance me now!

Step Three

Say all the wonderful things you want to re-introduce into

your life, and write them down if it will help you.

"Love...happiness...abundance....joy...health....laughter"

Whatever you want in your life state it now.

Herbs for Clearing

I have included the herbs for clearing here that I know about.

There are many more than these. With any kind of herb there is a 'right use'. I use the herbs that I know bring about the most healing and clearing, and, in my experience, are safe.

Sage

The spirit of Sage brings many gifts. It is a powerful clearing tool and enhances psychic gifts by keeping your cords clear of other people's energies and allows you to feel your own energy and become more attuned. Sage clears thoughts, the mind, other people's energies off of a person, thing, or place. It clears non-breathing Earth Bound Spirits that have not crossed over.

The smoke of the Sage carries prayers up to Creator. It clears so powerfully that pregnant women, women who are breastfeeding, and those with asthma or other sickness that affects breathing **should stay away from sage** so that no harm come to them. Put your prayers into the sage. White sage is masculine 'Grandfather' sage. The plains sage is 'Grandmother' sage, I have also seen it called Blue sage–and it is stringier. There are other types as well. I recommend the Grandfather and Grandmother Sage. Before burning any herb make sure it is safe for you.

Sweetgrass

Sweetgrass is by far my favorite herb for healing. The smoke of sweetgrass brings a sense of calming, relief, and restores good thoughts and mental balance. Sweetgrass is the medicine of changing someone's mind from sadness to happiness. It is a trickster of the very best kind. When you are sad, burn the sweetgrass. When you are happy burn the sweetgrass. When someone needs to remember how to laugh, burn the sweetgrass and laugh, laugh, laugh, and sing.

When we are born, we are born into a negative loop. Our bodies seek balance every day-oxygen to breathe, nourishment to live, social, and emotional comforts. That balancing act is called homeostatis. It is our daily adventure to find peace and happiness and maintain positivity and good belief systems. Use sweetgrass to call the good spirits and to manifest high vibrations of goodness, and restore gratitude.

Fill up the sadness holes with good things quickly – Sweetgrass is a good remedy for restoring the sweetness back into life. Before burning any herb make sure it is safe for you.

Osha Root (Bear Root)

This medicine came to me during sweat lodge, it is bitter and used for purification. When I started working with Osha I discovered it has so many good qualities. It works directly with life force energy–increasing life energy. It powerfully wards off malevolent energies. It helps increase personal power. Burn the smoke to help stay clear. Before burning any herb make sure it is safe for you.

Palo Santo

I use Palo Santo smoke to clear internal possessions. It works to clear anything attached to the upper part of the body. For this reason, some people use it as a remedy for headaches and migraines. Palo Santo is a medicine similar to sage, but has its own properties. It is a wood, however burns much like an herb. It heals lower vibrations and raises up the frequency so the person can clear. Burn it often in the winter, and during any form of chaos/crisis. It has a sweet smell, and is the medicine of love. It is a powerful protection.

Lavender

I have heard that lavender is woman's medicine, and I have heard that lavender is men's medicine (because it calms them and restores peace and their feminine nature). Lavender is both. That is why it is a very good medicine. It calms energies. Stress weakens the immune system. Calm enhances health and aids in healing. I use lavender in many of the holy waters I make. I use lavender in salt bath mixtures. Women know the lavender better than anyone, and have been using it for years and years for pregnancy, labor, and so many other reasons. I put the lavender in the sage dish and burn it with the sage. Lavender tea is also nice. Leaving lavender in a pouch in an area of a home where there is disharmony helps the members of the house to embrace harmony. Lavender helps women with mothering, child bearing, and for cleansing. Lavender helps men and women get along. Lavender helps reconnect to Great Spirit.

Incense

When burning incense, I always ask the Divine to 'come in' to the smoke no matter what type. For clearing I use Frankincense, Sage scent, Dragons blood, Lavender scented. There are many other scents that work for clearing. Go to what you are called. Smoke clears people, places, pets (with caution) and keeps energies clear.

Cedar

Cedar is not so much a clearing medicine as it is a positive vibration and healing medicine–so because it induces clear thoughts, it works to release the hold that other people's opinions have over you. It restores you to your core, your personal power to do your work and when you do this you heal. Cedar is a magical healing tool, I cannot describe how it has helped me and others, I only know it does. The medicine of Cedar is strength, and stability. It harmonizes and builds bridges–and gets you where you are trying to go. Burn the cedar in with sage to aid in clearing and helping direct a positive direction in life. Pray to the Cedar tree to repair broken homes, broken families, broken people, broken communities. Hang the Cedar branch over the front door of a home for good health. Put the cedar in your medicine bag and wear it for healing, strength, protection from sickness.

Crystals for Clearing

Information about the crystals listed here are based on my own personal experience, and may differ from other accounts of their metaphysical properties. These properties are not all inclusive nor meant to be a total account of the stones metaphysical properties. I have listed information based on what I have experienced, seen, heard, and felt. This is not a complete list, there are many stones that help with clearing.

Malachite

Malachite helps a person to stop over nurturing and detoxes them from unhealthy codependent relationships. It helps release patterns that are unhealthy and lead to taking on negative energies of other people. It is good to help with exorcisms and clearing because it will help identify where toxic energy is coming from and where it is being held in the physical body. Malachite helps to release anger from over nurturing and anxiety and stress from over doing it in life to help a person find the right balance and right focus.

Labradorite

This beautiful stone helps to open the vortex of light and direct energy where you want it to go. Because of this it is a fabulous stone to aid in purification, spirit releasement, to strengthen cord cutting. Labradorite helps you to open your crown chakra and connect to the Christ Ray and the Guidance offered to you. It helps you to set good intentions and aids in balancing your energy during clearing work. It is known to help bring peace to warring tribes and territorial disputes. It brings peace.

Crystal Quartz

The clear crystal vibration says it all—clear! Wearing a clear crystal will not only aid you in your work to clear others—it will help keep your mind clear. With mental clarity, a person is more closely connected to Creator, has stronger clairaudience, and clairvoyance. Quartz comes in many variations—Tibetan Quartz is my favorite for its clearing and healing properties. It aids to clear a person on the spiritual, mental, and psychic levels and helps them connect to their personal crystalline frequency and hold the most benevolent vibration of God's love and God's power.

Rose quartz

Rose quartz is used for many other reasons—however in clearing work it works by connecting to the vibration of Jesus. Rose quartz helps to hold the vibration of unconditional love—and brings darkness to light for purification. It helps you to keep your heart open and to remain compassionate to other people and to your own needs as well. Keep large pieces of Rose Quartz around you and think of Jesus often.

Amethyst

I wonder if there would have been an Amityville horror if there had been amethyst in that house? A terrible joke, however I seriously wondered it. Amethyst is powerful psychic protection. When there is bad energy and it goes ignored it turns into a monster all by itself. Turning your attention to protection is often a quick stop to a bad situation. Amethyst protects against addiction, and ultimately lies a demon or non-breathing Earth Bound Spirit or alien has been telling. It connects to truth–and truth is God. Amethyst is a wonderful stone for mental clarity, however it must "breathe" amethyst wants to be out in the open (however sometimes will be happy in a medicine bag) whenever possible–not tucked away. It helps people to face the truth, and the courage to clear what's been blocking you from it. Amethyst helps in better decision making. It helps to clear property, cats, and psychic attacks.

Smokey Quartz

The dark and beautiful Smokey quartz–your best helper in clearing dark energetics, malevolence, and negativity in all its forms. Smokey Quartz helps to move souls to where they need to be, and remove souls from where they do not belong. It helps to clear loved ones to Heaven, and keeps a practioner clear by directing negative energy away and releases negative energetics down to earth (or to heaven if that is where it is directed to go by God). Smokey helps protect dreams from psych pomp (another person or entity coming into your energy or your dreams) and is protection from demons and possession. It will aid to get the devil out of a person, place, or thing because it brings the light back in.

Bismuth

I discovered the healing properties of raw bismuth crystals many years ago when working with people experiencing grief and loss. I was guided to place a medium sized bismuth crystal on the chest or abdomen of clients. I discovered it 'takes' the sick emotions. It absorbs and it does not seem to have an end to how much it can take on—because of this exercise great care when using it, and clear it with cool water, and fresh air after using it for helping someone to release emotional build up—especially grief. In the years I have worked with others I have witnessed how deep sadness can leave doors open to malevolent energies—often releasing the sadness and grief will lead a person naturally back to a lighter and happier path in life.

Angelite

This beautiful stone helps you to feel, hear, and receive guidance from the benevolent Angelic realm. Wear it to feel lighter and more connected. It aids in centering and helps anyone who has lost their connection to God to find it again.

Carnelian

This ancient Egyptian stone is known to help psychopomp (travel) a person's soul to heaven or the Violet Ray. It is a powerful protection tool and worn by healers who know its powers. It keeps dark energetics away, and off the physical. It wards off malevolence from 'following you home' and keeps harmful energies at bay. It has a mysterious power, and harnesses the sacral chakra power to create. Worn during exorcisms you will most likely see positive results, feel strengthened in your faith, and experience less lingering after effects.

A Simple Crystal Clearing Technique:

Wear a clear quartz crystal as close to the top of your head (earrings or necklace) as possible for clarity and Divine Guidance. Wear a rose quartz as close to your heart as possible for focus 'in the now' and keeping your heart Open. Wear a Smoky Quartz to ground out negative energy that comes into your field as close to your heart (mid-section is okay), with the tip pointing down at the ground.

These three worn together provide a very nice balanced feeling while doing any Spiritual clearing work.

Rules for Dowsing With A Pendulum

It is very useful to use a pendulum to dowse for answers that help discern what is needed during a clearing. Muscle testing is another form of dowsing using the body. Without proper boundaries and limits placed on a Pendulum–it is no different than a Ouija Board (the word Ouija has so much negative energy on it I would not use a Ouija Board especially one made by someone else under any conditions).

Likewise, our bodies are no different than a pendulum or a Ouija Board and our bodies are fully capable of dowsing as well (hence muscle testing). That is why permissions and boundaries must be set, in order to use ANYTHING to dowse with.

Take your pendulum and clear it by sweeping energy off of it (pull the energy down and off of it with your hand, using a sweeping motion). You may also wash it in cool water, sage it, place it overnight under a full moon, or give it a salt bath.

Then say out loud:

Only my benevolent Angels and Guides,
the Archangels and God
may come through this Pendulum.

Light is In this Pendulum, and Light Surrounds this Pendulum. I am in the Light and Information comes FROM the Light. Only Truth from the Light can come through this pendulum now, and forever.

This Pendulum is connected to Divine Source.
I claim NO malevolent harmful energies / entities /
archons / thought forms have any rights over this
Pendulum—and any rights that were ever given in the
seen and unseen, known and unknown by myself or
anyone else are hereby revoked.

Love and Light
And Positive Energy Fills the Air
In and Around Me

Breathe and feel your aura fill with positive energy. The permissions have been set!

There are many different teachings on how to use a Pendulum. I follow a very simple method:

Yes–it swings forward and backward

No–it swings side to side

And "More Information" –it goes in a circle.

Permissions and Boundaries
Over Your Body
(and Rules for Using Muscle Testing)

The body is a temple of itself. A house for the Spirit. Our bodies are Sacred. We must learn how to love, care for, and honor, treat right, set permissions and boundaries, and protect our sacred body.

My body is connected to Divine Source.
I claim NO malevolent harmful energies / entities / thought forms have any rights over my body—and any rights that were ever given to anything harmful to me, in the seen and unseen, known and unknown by myself or anyone else, are hereby revoked.

For Muscle testing, I use a very simple technique here also—stand straight and tall and ask your body a question then let your body lean either forward or backwards from the hips.

Let your body naturally sway.

Forwards means the answer is yes.

Backwards means the answer is no.

After setting permissions over your body, **use a pendulum or muscle testing** to discern the best action, the best food, and what is the best protection for your body, **according to your Divine connection!**

After the Exorcism

Anyone healing from any form of malevolent possession, after your release and rebirth into the light and blood of Christ, should then consider three things:

1) **Treat any lingering depression.** Talk to a counselor to keep yourself clear and continue to take actions to keep from any form of depression. Ask a counselor for assistance staying focused on **the now**, and staying balanced and positive in your life. Seek medical help for any medical problems. Make health a priority.

2) **Spiritual Fitness.** Do all the things Spiritually Fit people do–pray, exercise, eat healthy, go to church, participate in a spiritual community you are called to, meditate, answer your calling in life, take care of your responsibilities, do nice things for others, and stay sane.

3) **Have Faith and Believe.** Make 'believing' your daily goal–believe God is working in your life, believe good things will happen and are happening now, take responsibility for your mental health and have a positive outlook. Believe something good every day.

These are the additional
tried and true techniques that I know to work.

I use them again and again and they work always:

Light 7 day candles and ask God (and the Saints and Angels and Archangels) to release from you, and lift off of you, any remaining negative energy, and ask God to fill your home with love and good energy.

Give away or Burn any item that has malevolent energy on it (harming no one and no thing or home). Use a pendulum to dowse what needs to be gotten rid of–trust 100% that God is helping you if something needs to go–it needs to go.
***Make sure to set the proper intentions before using any pendulum or dowsing tool (see Prayer page 207) that only

your benevolent guides and angels and God can come through your pendulum. Never use a pendulum if you are feeling you are not clear. Say the Clearing Prayers.

Smudge yourself daily, as well as your home, using sage and sweet grass. Sage is for clearing; sweet grass is for bringing in positive energy and Good Spirits.

Take salt showers or baths by taking regular table salt and rubbing it all over your body and letting then washing it off– make sure to get the crown of your head, all the way to the soles of your feet.

Play beautiful music.

Do wonderful things.

Bring home fresh flowers.

Feel good, burn nice smelling incense.

Buy something to remind you that you are healed—a picture of Jesus, a crystal, a positive saying about God.

Do gratitude work—say gratitude prayers, and be grateful—let your attitude reflect your gratitude.

Speak kind words—to yourself and others.

Hydrate yourself with good water, and nourish yourself with good food.

Receive the Word of God.

Stay humble.

Continue to Receive Healing.

Stay in the Now.

Pray.

Epilogue

Every Spiritual Person who works with others should be able to know what to do in the event you encounter a possessed person. In all likelihood, you will.

The level of possession and type of possession can only be ruled by a chosen worker of God. You can usually tell these people by their dress, their demeanor, humility, code of conduct, and their professional Spiritual appearance.

They say ignorance is bliss. For wise people – ignorance is unavailable. Armor is what's available.

During the writing of this little book I encountered intense trials. I slept with the lights on, I prayed intensely and took a walk of faith I didn't know was possible.

Every step of the way I was protected, I was strengthened, I was given the tools I needed to stay healthy, safe, and unscathed.

In the process of writing this book I had some people say things like "if you believe it is there it is there–so just believe it is not there and it will go away".

I too have Buddhist beliefs such as these–and have wondered many times why the Spiritually sick keep showing up in my life.

One day I received the answer: "If there was a speck in your eye would you not take it out? Or would you ignore it is there and pretend you can see perfectly". (Thank you Master Buddha).

When someone comes to you for help if you ignore the speck–you have done them a great disservice. Hence, I have written this book. We must always stay vigilant to the highest positive vibration possible–and when you get there

God will surely put you to work helping others who are not there.

Negative energies, and 'psychic attacks' affect your energy, your vision, your discernment, your mood, and your physical, mental, and emotional health.

Today, a candle is burning for anyone who is experiencing spiritual attack or spiritual sickness.

When you feel week, when you feel anxiety, when you feel heavy with burdens, when you feel sick, when you feel depressed, when you feel self-loathing, and when you feel what you are going through is inescapable—the candle is burning for you, and it will never go out.

About the Author

Kass Huff, Psychic Medium

A LIVING BRIDGE TO THE BEYOND

Kass Huff is a sought after naturally gifted Psychic Medium, Psychic Investigator, Medical Intuitive, Healer, Animal Communicator, Instructor, and Empowerment Coach who is connected to the 4 winds and Great Spirit. A living bridge to the beyond, bringing you messages *for your Spirit*.

Kass offers offers Readings, Communication with Loved Ones and Pets, Astrology Reports, Animal Communication,

Healing Sessions, Hypnotherapy & Past Life
Regressions, Business and Love Coach, Psychic
Investigations, Paranormal Assistance
and House Clearings. Kass Reads
for People all over the World.

Kass began working with her gifts after helping the family of
a missing person. She continues to help on cases,
with investigators, and law enforcement as she is able to
help. She currently reads for people all over the world,
channels, teaches, and assists with paranormal investigations
and missing persons cases as able. Pro Bono for Law
Enforcement.

Kass is available for readings by phone, in person and house
calls. Pro Bono for Law Enforcement.

Kass offers therapeutic God's Light Reiki Healing,
and Shamanic Healing Sessions–and teaches classes.

All the services Kass offers are by appointment and may be
booked weeks in advance.

If you are someone you know is spiritually sick—now is the time to get healed.

Call 253-503-6816 or 360-458-5515

or Contact info@kasshuff.com.

www.kasshuff.com

Earthly Oasis

Tranquil Sanctuary of Wellness and Health

Gift Store, Readings, Healing, and Classes

www.earthlyoasis.com

Find Earthly Oasis on Etsy
https://www.etsy.com/shop/EarthlyOasis

For information about

Spiritual Fitness Foundation Retreats

Visit

www.SpiritualFitnessFoundation.org

For information about

Tacoma Paranormal Research Society

Visit

https://www.facebook.com/Tacoma-Paranormal-Research-Society-856948547780292/